The student's guide
to research ethics

The student's guide to research ethics

Paul Oliver

Open University Press
Maidenhead · Philadelphia

Open University Press
McGraw-Hill Education
McGraw-Hill House
Shoppenhangers Road
Maidenhead
Berkshire
England
SL6 2QL

email: enquiries@openup.co.uk
world wide web: www.openup.co.uk

and

325 Chestnut Street
Philadelphia, PA 19106, USA

First published 2003

A catalogue record of this book is available from the British Library

ISBN 0 335 21087 2 (pb)   0 335 21088 0 (hb)

Library of Congress Cataloging-in-Publication Data
Oliver, Paul, 1946–   .
    The student's guide to research ethics / Paul Oliver.
        p.   cm.
    Includes bibliographical references and index.
    ISBN 0–335–21088–0 – ISBN 0–335–21087–2 (pbk.)
    1. Research – Moral and ethical aspects.   I. Title.

    Q180.55.M67 O38   2003
    174'.90901 – dc21   2002042574

Typeset by RefineCatch Limited, Bungay, Suffolk
Printed in Great Britain by Bell and Bain Ltd, Glasgow

Contents

PART 1
Ethics and the research process

1 Introduction
Ethics and research

Research in the social sciences is often concerned with collecting data from people. Almost inevitably this raises questions about the way in which people who provide data should be treated by researchers, and such questions are often ethical in nature. The research community is becoming increasingly more sophisticated in the manner in which it considers such ethical issues, and there appears to be a growing concern with the ethical dimension of planning and implementing research.

This book tries to explore such issues as they occur throughout the research process. It is intended to be of use to higher education students in education and the social sciences, who are conducting a research project. It is hoped that it will be of particular help to postgraduate students with their theses, and also as a resource for lecturers. The book includes a number of fictional 'ethical dilemmas' and 'ethical dialogues' to indicate the contextual nature of ethical issues. In addition, a range of theoretical perspectives are integrated with the text, in order to explore how these may illuminate ethical problems in research.

Some terminological issues: participants, subjects or respondents?

When I am advising my own students on writing up their research, one of my standard pieces of advice is, 'make certain you define your terms'. As subject areas, both ethics and research contain some potentially complex concepts, and much of this book will be concerned with trying to clarify them. Perhaps we can start with one or two commonly used terms in research.

Social science research data may exist in a variety of forms. The data may be collected directly as during an interview, or while observing a group of people. Alternatively, the data may consist of artefacts produced by people, such as a diary or, perhaps more unconventionally, the contents of a waste bin in an office. In research literature, there are a number of terms which are used to describe people who provide data, such as research subjects, participants or respondents, or sometimes a term such as interviewee, to reflect the particular data-collection method which has been employed. At first sight, the terms which we use to describe people who provide data may seem relatively unimportant, but the concepts used do carry implications for how we view people and their role in the research process. The word 'subject' perhaps carries the implication that something is being done *to* them, while the term 'participant' implies that something is being carried out in conjunction *with* them. During the research process, the distinction could be quite important.

Not only are there issues to clarify about the people who provide data, but also the terms used to describe researchers reflect the differing roles occupied by those who collect and analyse data. There are first of all people who are full-time, professional researchers. Such people may work for a commercial organization, for example in market research, or they may be attached to a university. They may be research students working towards a research degree, or research fellows or associates working on a funded research project. A large amount of the work reported in academic journals is conducted by people who are carrying out research as an integral part of their professional lives. University lecturers are perhaps an obvious example, but there is an increasing number of other professionals who view research as an important part of their job and of their professional development. These include school teachers, managers, social workers, health care professionals and community workers. Sometimes, where such professionals are also involved in research, their joint role is signified in the literature by the use of a hyphen, as in 'teacher-researcher'. There may be occasions, however, where the joint roles may conflict to some extent, or where careful thought must be exercised about competing obligations. We need therefore to look at these joint roles, and to explore areas where ethical issues could arise.

Having explored the problem of terminology in brief, let us return to those who provide data. Perhaps the most traditional term in use here is 'subject'. The use of this term is more commonly associated with research which tends to reflect the approach of the natural sciences such as physics and chemistry. Such research can be said to be carried out within a positivistic paradigm. It is perhaps typified by the use of an experimental model for research, where the researcher tries to control the majority of variables, while manipulating only one or two of them. Experimental research is found in disciplines such as psychology, social psychology, management and organization studies, and in communication studies. If a research study is being conducted on the social behaviour of employees in a company, the research report may well refer to them as 'employees'. Similarly, in research on the process of children learning to read, the report may refer to those providing data as 'the children'. Where the term 'subject' is used, however, as in for example

Wattenmaker (2000) we have to be aware that the concept carries some implications of how a hypothetical researcher may view the members of the research sample. The term subject perhaps carries the suggestion that members of the sample have a rather passive role in the research programme; that they have agreed to provide data or perhaps to be tested as part of a research project. There is a suggestion that apart from providing data, the 'subjects' of the research have little or no role to play in the research programme, and are relegated to a minor role in the proceedings. As research subjects we perhaps develop the feeling that they will not interact very much with those actually doing the research, and will concern themselves solely with their function of providing data.

The disadvantage from an ethical point of view, of the use of the term subject, is that arguably it tends to depersonalize the members of the sample, and reduce them to a subservient role in the research process. This is not to suggest that this happened in the article mentioned earlier, merely that it may be an implicit danger. It is important to remember that we are discussing the social or *human* sciences, and hence should do everything possible to retain a sense of dignity and worth for everyone involved in the research process. It could be argued that the more we tend to forget the humanity of our research sample members, the greater the possibility (however slight) that researchers might use procedures which are less than ethical. It might be useful to explore the use of the concept 'subject' in terms of one of the arguments of the philosopher Immanuel Kant (1724–1804: see Box 1.1).

Box 1.1   Theoretical perspective: the categorical imperative

Kant argued that when we are choosing how we should act under certain circumstances, we should apply criteria which are capable of becoming universal principles. In other words, under comparable circumstances, other people could apply the same principles. Kant termed this approach to ethical problems the categorical imperative (see O'Neill 1993: 175–85).

Now this may seem to be a fine point, but some feel that the use of the term 'subject', reduces, in a rather subtle way, the status of the person providing the data. It may be felt that the term suggests a slight lack of respect for the individual as a person or human being. Perhaps we could argue here that there is a universal principle involved, and that this principle involves treating all those involved in the research process equally. In other words, the researcher is no more important than the person providing data; they merely have different roles in the enterprise of research. This then becomes a categorical imperative, and we should hence always select terminology which reflects this principle of equality of treatment. The problem is, of course, that two people may agree with the principle of equality of treatment, but differ as to whether the term 'subject' reflects a sense of inequality.

The use of the word 'subject' appears to imply that the research process is unidirectional, that it proceeds from the researcher to the 'subject'. The researcher initiates proceedings, which then have an impact upon the 'subject'. Arguably, this is much less true of the term 'respondent'. In everyday language when we speak of someone 'responding to a request' there is a sense in which the person is able to choose whether or not to respond. There is an element of volition in the process. The use of the term respondent in research does tend to underline the autonomy of the person providing the data. There is the suggestion of a person with a much more active role to play. From the point of view of research ethics, the term respondent appears to be a much more satisfactory term than subject. It retains a sense of the free will of the person providing data, and suggests, by implication, that if the circumstances of the research were not entirely satisfactory to the respondent that they might withdraw cooperation.

The term respondent is certainly widely used in research articles (see for example Brown et al. 2000; Denscombe 2001). The same articles also use another popular term to refer to members of the research sample, and that is 'participant'. Whereas the term respondent may give the impression of some-one who while providing data is not closely involved in the research process, the concept participant suggests a different kind of relationship. If we speak of a person participating in an activity, such as for example the organization of a social event, there is the assumption that the person is fully involved in the process. We assume that the person is involved in planning and decision-making, and in the execution of the plan. In research terms, when we reflect on the role of the participant, we certainly envisage a role which is more extensive than that of simply providing data. There is the implication that the person is perhaps consulted over certain matters, such as the organization of the data collection, at least in so far as it affects the participant. We may not necessarily envisage participants taking an active part in the research design, or having a role which is equal to that of the researcher, but there is certainly a feeling of a much more democratic involvement than in the case of the term respondent.

One might tend to associate the term participant with a qualitative or interpretative research perspective. The reason for this is that such perspectives place a great emphasis upon the unique contribution of each individual to the collective nature of society. They stress the individual vision of the world, a view which appears to be in harmony with the idea of the individual sample member who is also invited to contribute to the overall research strategy. Nevertheless, the association with interpretative research is by no means an absolute rule, and some quantitative studies retain the use of the term 'participants' (see for example Cameron and Lalonde 2001).

The use of the pair of terms, 'interviewer' and 'interviewee', is also popular in social science research circles. In fact, it was employed in the already mentioned Denscombe (2001) article. The advantage of using a pair of terms such as these is that one appears to avoid the attribution of value judgements to either term: there does not appear to be the same assumption of a power and status differential as in the case of 'researcher/subject'. The very similarity of the terms interviewer and interviewee tends to suggest a parity of status. The term interviewee also has the advantage of conveying the type of data-collection method used.

There is an alternative to the use of these terms when referring to the members of the research sample, however, and that is to describe the people concerned using a broad category. This technique was again used by Denscombe, who referred to his sample on more than one occasion as consisting of 'young people'. If the descriptive term is chosen carefully, and reflects accurately the category of people in the sample, then it should not imply any value or status differentials between the researcher and those who provide data. It should in principle, be a value-neutral term. So, if the sample consists of headteachers, we refer to them as headteachers; if the sample consists of social workers, then we refer to them as such. Whichever term we prefer, when writing a research report, it may be necessary to use alternatives simply to retain a freshness of writing style. In this book I have tended to alternate between the use of participant and respondent, depending upon the context and which term seemed to be more appropriate. Perhaps the main issue is that we try to be sensitive to the possible connotations of words, and try to select our terms carefully.

Moving from those who provide data to those who collect it, there are perhaps rather fewer problems of nomenclature. If a term is used at all, then 'researcher' often suffices, and does not generally suggest any value judgements. In some areas of research, however, there is an increasing tendency for the role of the researcher to be linked with a professional role. This may lead to terms such as the 'practitioner-researcher' or more commonly, with education, the 'teacher-researcher', for example, in the case of school teachers conducting research within their own classrooms or schools. The term could well be adapted to the 'nurse-researcher' or the 'social-worker-researcher'. The purpose of the research may be to gain a higher degree or research degree, or perhaps for professional development and ultimately of publishing an article in a scholarly journal.

The combination of the professional role and of the researcher role may, however, lead to a lack of certainty about the separation of the roles, or perhaps to a conflict of interests. An issue which can arise fairly commonly is whether activities involved in the collection of data could be construed to be a part of the teacher's normal professional role. Consider, for example, the ethical dilemma described in Box 1.2.

Box 1.2 Ethical dilemma: permission to collect data

You are a teacher of biology in a high school. You are interested in conducting research on the attitudes of your students to field trips, and whether they feel that fieldwork helps their understanding of scientific concepts. You wonder whether it is necessary to seek formal permission to collect data on the opinions of your students, since this seems to be a part of your normal job.

This example is definitely an *ethical* dilemma because it is concerned with how one *ought* to behave in both a professional and research context. The teacher here is rightly concerned to ensure that the research role is not merging with the teacher role in an unacceptable manner. If, for example, the teacher started to interview the students and ask them questions about their views of field trips, would the students feel that it was inappropriate in some way? A teacher, like any professional, has a role which is circumscribed by the terms of their contract, by custom and practice, and by the norms and values which have evolved within the social context of that school. To move outside the limits of those conventions may not be explicitly contrary to the teacher's contract, but it may cause concern, disquiet or anxiety in the students. This is not an argument for conformity, but merely to suggest that it is important to have a concern for the feeling of students.

It may not be very common for a teacher to interview students about their feelings about field trips, and hence to start doing so without a careful introduction may be seen as inappropriate. There may not be anything wrong with collecting data on student attitudes, especially given the current extent of evaluation practices throughout the education system. Students are becoming familiar with being asked their opinions about various aspects of the teaching and learning process. However, the students should be approached in such a way that they are given a full explanation of the research and its purposes. (More will be said in discussion of 'informed consent' in Chapter 2.) Thus, one might argue that if the students are briefed on the purpose of the data collection, and they are happy to proceed, there is no further obligation to obtain permission. The research is so close to the kind of evaluation of teaching and courses which has become common practice that any further seeking of permission may be unnecessary.

This may not be the case, however, if the teacher intends to write up and publish the research, when a different range of ethical obligations arise. It would be important to ensure that the students understood the way in which the teacher intended to use the data which they provided, and that they approved of that use. (For a discussion of the teacher-researcher role, see Middlewood et al. 1999.)

Thus we can see that the terminology used for both the researcher and the persons providing data has implications for the ethics of the research process. The terms which we decide to use for the providers of data carry implicit assumptions about the way in which we view them. Equally, if we employ a term such as teacher-researcher, there are assumptions about the way in which those two roles interact.

Ethics and research aims

It is important to consider ethical issues from the early stages of a research project. From the beginning of the design process, provisional decisions are usually taken about the nature of the research sample, and of the methodology. Inevitably these decisions imply certain ways of interacting with the people involved in the research project. Researchers often try to express the anticipated goals of the research in terms of research aims, and the latter often highlight potential ethical issues. For example, consider two school teachers who would like to explore the connection, if any, between levels of school attendance of students, and the levels of achievement in examinations at age 16. As they plan their research, and draft their research aims, they begin to discuss the ethical issues involved in using existing school data (see Box 1.3).

Box 1.3 Ethical dialogue: using existing statistical data

Teacher A: Of course, there wouldn't be any problem with data; we've got it all on file. We've certainly got the exam results for years back, and with a bit of luck, loads of registers too.

Teacher B: What about getting permission though? Especially with regard to attendance, but exam results too for that matter.

Teacher A: Yes, but we'll aggregate the data. That way it's impossible for anyone to be identified.

Teacher B: OK, I see that. But it would only give us very broad trends. We might want to take a few students as case studies. You know, individuals who are exceptional in some way. They might have missed a lot of classes, but still done well.

Teacher A: That's a good advert for our teaching!

Teacher B: We'd have to either guarantee them anonymity, or get a variety of permissions.

Teacher A: Or both.

Teacher B: Let's make a list of the people we might need to consult.

What the teachers have probably discovered is that it is never too early to be thinking about ethical issues when planning research! It is the kind of subject that the more you think about it, the more issues come into your mind.

The two teachers have explored an interesting issue. They seem to be working their way towards the conclusion that when many separate items of data are aggregated, and since this process obscures individual identity, then it is less important to obtain permission to use the data. On the other hand, when larger quantities of data about a single person are used, then obtaining permission becomes much more significant. This is where the connection with the aims of a research project becomes rather more important.

The aims of a piece of research may involve making large-scale comparisons between groups of human beings or between a number of organizations at the same time. Where this is so, the ethics of the situation may be a little less demanding, since data can be combined, and thus individual identity obscured. On the other hand, if in a piece of ethnographic or field research, the aim is to explore the life histories of a relatively small number of individuals, then it may be more important to ensure that they understand the purpose and function of the research, before agreeing to take part. Certainly, when researchers write the aims of a project, those aims do tend to imply certain forms of methodology and of data collection. In turn, these raise particular ethical issues. In other words, it is at the stage of preparing the aims of a research project that the researcher could be well advised to first consider research ethics.

Moral justifications of research

If we were to ask people what they thought was the main purpose of research, many of the responses might be concerned with 'adding to the sum total of human knowledge', or 'to get a better understanding of the universe', or 'to gain knowledge of the way the world works'. There would clearly be other answers, but it seems likely that many would involve the notion of acquiring knowledge as being at the heart of the research enterprise.

Now the acquisition of knowledge raises an interesting ethical question which can be framed as, 'is the gaining of knowledge about the world a good thing?' There are many straightforward instances, where we would probably answer with an unreserved 'yes'. We might think of medical research where a scientist discovers a new treatment for a disease, or of engineering research, where an engineer discovers how to make an inexpensive type of water pump which could be used to help drought-inflicted areas in the developing world. A sociologist might conduct research on deprived housing estates, and so inform a better government policy on inner-city housing, or an educationalist might develop a new way of assessing school pupils which is fairer than the one previously used.

However, suppose we examined a range of research in the social sciences, which, while very interesting, had never been put to any practical use. It had, perhaps, added slightly to our understanding of society, but it seemed unlikely that it could be used to enhance the quality of life of people. How would we feel about that? Would we feel that such research was a 'good' thing? I suspect we would generally feel that it was a 'good' thing, but we might feel slightly less enthusiastic about it.

What then about a chemical engineer who researches and discovers a new method of dispersing micro-organisms to use as biological weapons? Would we feel that this knowledge was 'good'. This becomes rather more difficult. Some might say that such knowledge is simply undesirable, and we would be better off without ever having acquired it. Others might want to distinguish, however, between the knowledge itself, and the uses to which it might be put. In other words, they might argue that there is never anything wrong with knowledge per se, only with the uses to which it might be put by certain ill-intentioned people. Such an argument is coming very close to the distinction made by philosophers between something which is good *intrinsically* and something which is good *instrumentally*. Let us briefly examine the difference (see Box 1.4).

Box 1.4   Theoretical perspective: intrinsic and instrumental good

An intrinsic good is an entity which is commonly regarded as noble and virtuous, because of its fundamental qualities and characteristics. 'Justice' and 'truth-telling' may be examples of intrinsic goods. On the other hand, the existence of an efficient police force in a country may be regarded as an instrumental good, since it may be a key instrument in ensuring justice for the citizens. Sometimes, an intrinsic good may not be instrumentally good. Consider person A, who is looking for person B to do them harm. You know the location of person B. If person A asks you where person B is, and you tell the truth because you want to do the intrinsic good, the result may be very unpleasant for person B (see Railton 1998: 170).

So our key question is whether the acquisition of knowledge through research is an intrinsic good or an instrumental good, or perhaps a combination of the two depending upon the circumstances. Certainly, it seems difficult to imagine a situation where we might want to draw a line and say that now we have sufficient knowledge about the world. After all, we do not know what situations are going to arise in the future, and we may well need new knowledge to cope with those situations. This kind of thought might incline us to the notion that knowledge, and hence research, are intrinsically good, but others might take a different view!

There is a related question concerned with the overall purposes of research. Even if we were to accept that research to acquire knowledge was an intrinsic good, we may not be prepared to accept a situation where research seldom helped to improve the lot of human beings; we might have reservations about such a situation. We may have to resign ourselves to the notion that new knowledge may be used for both good and ill. This may be particularly true of scientific and technological advances and can also be true of research in the social sciences. Research on human intelligence, designed to help children learn more effectively, may later be employed by others to treat less favourably those people who are deemed to be less able intellectually.

Perhaps the key issue is that in order to place research on a firm moral footing, there should at least be the *intent* to improve the human condition. Researchers will eventually, through the process of publication, make their results available in the public domain, and thenceforward cannot guarantee that they will not be put to some inappropriate use. Nevertheless, perhaps we can consider this as a moral criterion for all research.

One problem with an intent criterion is that we would have to accept the assessment of different people that a particular research project would be likely to benefit humanity. Suppose that a researcher is investigating aspects of unemployment, and has the expressed intention of developing policies which may help unemployed people in gaining employment. Other people, however, suggest there is evidence that this kind of research programme tends to categorize people as 'the unemployed' and in effect stigmatizes them and tends to adversely affect their self-image. The researcher is not persuaded by this, however, and persists with the research on the grounds that they have the intent of improving the lot of those who are unemployed.

Well, perhaps there are two alternatives here. We may conclude that the acquisition of knowledge is a sufficient good in itself, and it requires no further moral justification in terms of the intention of the researcher. On the other hand, we may consider it unacceptable that research exists in a kind of moral vacuum, where the researcher does not reflect upon their aims and intentions. If we are persuaded by the latter principle, we may wish it to be a universal criterion that researchers at least try, through their work, to enhance the conditions of life.

Situations where engaging in research may be ethically undesirable

In all research involving the collection of data from human beings, there is a fundamental moral requirement to treat those people in accord with standards and values which affirm their essential humanity. The research context is really no different in this respect from any other context in which human interaction takes place. Most people I think would agree that as human beings we should be treated according to certain criteria by other human beings, and that equally we should treat others according to those same criteria. The problem, of course, as in many aspects of ethics, is that there may not be complete agreement about all of those criteria. However, there may be reasonable agreement about some of them.

We may feel, for example, that in any form of human interaction, including research, human beings should not be physically or mentally cruel to each other, they should respect each other's privacy, and they should not interfere with each other's freedom of action (within certain limits). These general assumptions about how we ought to relate to other human beings, create certain broad parameters which define the kinds of research activities which are acceptable, and those which are less acceptable or even unacceptable.

In order to illustrate and analyse some of these issues let us consider a discussion between two researchers who are planning a research project on potentially substandard housing conditions in an inner-city area. They want to visit a number of families living in a fairly deprived area, and to gather data on the living conditions in those houses. They discuss how they might first contact families to take part in the research (see Box 1.5).

The act of contacting participants in a research study may not seem too complicated at first sight, but this discussion reveals some subtleties in the situation. Researcher B highlights the need to act in a sensitive manner to potential participants, and to ensure as far as possible that we do not demean or belittle people. To suggest to people that the only reason they have been selected for the research study is that they live in what appears to be poor housing, may well be interpreted as demeaning and rather insulting. (For a discussion of recruiting respondents, see Maykut and Morehouse 1994: 56.)

The researchers discuss the possibility of telling potential participants that the survey is concerned with housing in general, in order to spare their feelings. The motive for this may be moral, but the action does not conform with the principle of giving participants full information about the project. Some people may simply not want to be associated with a research project which is looking at substandard housing. They may feel that it labels or stigmatizes them, and they may be concerned that friends and relatives may find out. This may not seem like a totally rational reaction to some researchers, but nevertheless, they are not in the position of the participants providing data. The researchers conclude, perhaps on balance correctly, that the advantage of a potentially less stressful introduction with respondents is not justified by the strategy of misleading them about the fact of the research concerning poorer housing.

Box 1.5   Ethical dialogue: contacting respondents

Researcher A: One way would be to define the boundaries of the area, and then take a random sample of the houses. If we select a fairly deprived area, we will get at least some poorly maintained houses.

Researcher B: OK, that would work; or we could simply drive round and make a note of houses which looked run down. But my problem is what do we do then? We can't very well just knock on the door and say we're doing a study of people living in poor housing. Not only would it be a bit of an insult, but they probably wouldn't want to help us then anyway.

Researcher A: It could easily lead to unpleasantness.

Researcher B: What if we wrote to them first, and said we would call at their house the following week? We could then say in the letter that this was a survey of housing in the area, without mentioning that it was about deprived housing.

Researcher A: We could do that, but I'm not too keen on the ethics of it. The whole point of the research is to examine inadequate housing, and if we don't explain that to people, then I'm not sure it's fair.

Researcher B: It's not, I agree. I was just trying to think of a pleasanter way to make the introductions.

Researcher A: Besides, we are going to have to tell people that there will be a report written, which will probably be on display in the public library. We will have to explain briefly the background to commissioning this research.

Researcher B: No one will be named though.

Researcher A: Well, I think people will need reassuring on that point.

Researcher B: Maybe we are approaching this the wrong way. The problem is that it is going to be difficult conveying all of this quickly, and we may miss out something important. Perhaps we should mailshot houses with a nice, interesting flyer about the research, and say everything in one go. At least we know they have had the information, and when we knock on the door it should not be too much of a surprise.

The researchers are reminded that a report will be produced on the research, and that even though individual participants will not be named, it will presumably be self-evident that the research was concerned with poorer housing. In other words, not only should people be fully informed about the research on purely ethical grounds, but also it should be recognized that if they are not informed for some reason, they may learn about the true nature of the research project at a later stage. Researcher A argues that participants will almost certainly need reassurance on the matter of their own anonymity in the research report. Many participants are understandably concerned about this. Even though they may be reassured by the researcher, they may still harbour residual uncertainties.

The strategy of posting a flyer to every house seems a sensible one, but it is hard to be certain that each householder will read the flyer, and internalize the contents. Given the large amount of mail which comes through everyone's letter box these days, it seems a little unfair to assume that each household will thereby be fully informed about the research project. However, it forms a reasonable basis upon which to have a further discussion with potential participants.

Let us summarize some of the issues which emerge from this dialogue, and which are concerned with preserving some essential elements of the humanity and dignity of participants. Research should avoid causing harm, distress, anxiety, pain or any other negative feeling to participants. Participants should be fully informed about all relevant aspects of the research, before they agree to take part. There is perhaps a discussion to be had about the scope of 'relevant aspects' and how 'relevant' is defined. Nevertheless there is a clear appreciation that if people do not understand the nature of the research project, they are not really in a position to give their fully informed agreement. Potential participants should be informed about the anticipated means of disseminating the research findings, and also about the way (if any) in which the research was commissioned, which may be significant if the research project has been funded by an organization known to potential participants. The scope of the confidentiality of the data provided, and of the anonymity of the respondents, particularly in any final research report, should be clarified with the participants. These are some of the important ways in which participants should be treated in order to help preserve their dignity. If one or more of such conditions are not met, then it does call into question the ethical acceptability of the research project. This discussion raises an interesting issue about ethical decision-making – the distinction between 'means' and 'ends' (see Box 1.6).

Box 1.6   Theoretical perspective: 'means' and 'ends'

If we wish to attain a particular goal in life, then we may refer to that as an 'end'. In order to achieve the 'end', we will almost certainly have to follow certain procedures or take certain action. That is referred to as the 'means'. If the end that we have in sight is to help the victims of an earthquake in a remote, mountainous region, then the means we employ may be to collect and transport a lot of warm, second-hand clothing and blankets. In this case, the means seems to be a sensible and moral method of achieving the end. In ethics, a dilemma can sometimes arise whereby we can identify a moral end, but are uncertain about the morality of the means we intend to use to achieve it (see Davis 1993: 210).

In the case about research into deprived housing, the researchers all along had a moral end in sight. They wanted to collect data on substandard housing in order to make out a case for improvements in the housing stock. However, they came across ethical problems when they tried to plan a means of collecting data. One of the means which they considered involved giving the impression that the research concerned housing in general, rather than substandard housing. They decided to reject this method on ethical grounds.

Responsibilities of researchers to fellow researchers, respondents, the public and the academic community

As we discussed earlier, research is concerned with extending the sum total of knowledge in society, and researchers are normally seen as occupying an important role. The general public probably views researchers as being intelligent and well educated, and perhaps adheres to the stereotype of the person in the white coat experimenting with the content of test tubes! This public perception of the researcher operating in a rather ethereal realm also brings with it certain assumptions about behavioural norms. These may include values such as truth-telling, accuracy of reporting findings, trying to make results understandable, and being honest about both the successes and failings of a research project. In short, the public respect for researchers brings with it certain responsibilities.

Similar principles tend to operate within the academic community. Among educational managers, teachers, lecturers and students, researchers are generally held in high esteem. The academic community also expects high ethical standards of behaviour. Let us start by considering the responsibilities of researchers to society at large.

It is important to bear in mind that much research associated with universities or funded by government grant is ultimately paid for with money raised by taxation, therefore members of the public have certain expectations of such research. Such expectations may also be conditioned by the fact that many of the people indirectly helping to pay for research are not themselves occupying jobs either as interesting or as well paid as those of researchers. It is not unreasonable if members of the public expect research to contribute to the public good. Given the wide range of topics in social research, one could argue that research should, wherever possible, focus upon problems whose resolution would improve the general quality of life. If there is a lot of drug-taking in an area, then assuming the required expertise is available, perhaps this should be designated as a priority area for research. If in a particular local education authority, boys in high school are tending not to achieve as well as girls, there may be a case for researching this with some urgency.

We should also not forget that members of the public are interested in the results of research if they are concerned with their daily lives. However, they will understandably wish to have the research reported in a manner which they can understand. Thus, whether it is during an interview on radio or television, or in a newspaper account, it is incumbent upon researchers to explain their research findings in a style which can be understood by most people, yet which does full justice to the academic content of the research. This may not always be easy to achieve, but the researcher should attempt to communicate with the audience who will be most affected by the research. It should be remembered that the research participants will have a vested interest in the research results, and they may not belong to the academic community. Consideration should also be given to ensuring that they have access to the research results in an understandable format. The researcher has diverse roles and aims which merge together, but it could be argued that one of the fundamental ones is to serve the public and to attempt to improve the general quality of life.

Apart from their responsibilities to the general public, researchers exist within a network of ethical obligations to other members of the academic community. There are a number of different jobs or roles within the academic community whose incumbents are to a greater or lesser extent involved in research. There are postgraduate research students, research fellows, professors, readers, contract researchers, lecturers, research assistants, deans, heads of department, academic journal editors and publishers. Most of these individual post-holders will have obligations and responsibilities to others in the list, depending upon their particular involvement in research. For example, a lecturer may have been awarded an internal research grant which is managed by the dean, and to whom the lecturer is accountable for expenditure on the research project. A reader may have written an article for a journal, and be responsible to the journal editor for proof-reading the article. Although these responsibilities may not have a specific ethical element, ethical issues are implicit within them. Many relationships within the academic community involve specific ethical issues. Consider for example the situation described in Box 1.7.

The research student's dilemma was whether to agree with the request. She was presumably proud of her first academic article, and understandably wanted the pleasure and kudos of seeing her name in print as the author. The key question is whether the request by the supervisor was reasonable. Let us first look at the issue from the supervisor's point of view.

The supervisor presumably felt that she had helped the student design the research for the doctorate and had provided guidance on the methodology. As this was the same methodology used to guide the data collection for both the article and the thesis, she perhaps felt that she had played a crucial role in the research reported in the article. In addition she had provided structural

---

Box 1.7 Ethical dilemma: authorship of journal articles

A research student is working towards her PhD in education, and has used some of the 'surplus' data from her doctoral research to write and submit a journal article. She sought advice from her supervisor while she was writing the article. Her supervisor provided advice on the general structuring of the article, and also read and commented on the first draft of the article. When the draft had been revised and was ready for submission, the supervisor suggested that her name should be added as a joint author. The student thought this over and eventually reluctantly agreed , although she retained a feeling that the request had not been entirely fair.

---

advice without which the researcher may never have written the article, and she had also made a critical contribution in terms of proof-reading the article. In short, she felt that she fully merited the status of joint author.

The research student, for her part, was in a difficult situation. She had always accepted the advice of her supervisor, and had grown to trust her judgement. However, she could not help her feelings that the request from her supervisor was slightly unfair. Her supervisor had not written any of the article, which was nearly 8000 words long. She had not advised her on the methodology, as that had come from the doctorate. As the supervisor was employed to advise on the doctorate, it did not seem to the student that it was reasonable to expect additional credit for that by being noted as a joint author. Although the supervisor had commented and advised on the overall structure of the paper, the student felt that she understood most of this from reading articles already published in the journal. The proof-reading had been a help, although in reality the comments had been relatively minor. On reflection, the student felt that she had been treated rather unfairly by the supervisor.

Now if the student felt like this, and also had the opportunity to think things over, why did she agree to include her supervisor as joint author? The answer to this presumably lies in the differential power relationship between supervisor and research student. The latter depends upon the supervisor for the management of the research degree, for helping to organize the examination arrangements, for providing detailed guidance on the final draft of the entire thesis, and generally for providing support through what is a difficult and at times stressful experience. It is not easy for a research student to oppose the advice of a supervisor, and certainly not easy to refuse a request in this kind of situation. One would conjecture that this was the most likely reason for the research student agreeing to a request about which she had reservations.

Well, if required, how would we arbitrate in such a situation? Was the request a fair one? In order to try to resolve the issue we perhaps need to analyse the different elements of the work involved in writing a research paper, and then to consider the contributions of the research student and of the supervisor.

There are two broad components in the writing of a research article. There is first the academic content, which may include the planning and design of the research, the analysis of previous literature, the act of data collection, and the intellectual element of the data analysis. The drawing of conclusions from the research is also an important element of this intellectual activity. Second, there is the separate but related issue of the work involved in the actual writing. This is the act of turning data and ideas into a piece of coherent writing.

In looking back at the respective contributions of the supervisor and of the student, it seems that with the exception of the minor proof-reading, the student had completed all of the writing aspect of the work. The supervisor had inevitably contributed something to the research design, but this was originally as part of the thesis supervision. Some advice had been given on the overall structure of the article, but it appears that this advice had not been extensive. We are then left with the impression that the majority of the work was that of the student. One might be forgiven for thinking that in these situations a fairly straightforward principle of fairness should apply. In other words, the manner of attribution of authorship should reflect the contribution to the article in terms of both ideas and writing. In this case it might perhaps seem more reasonable to append a note at the end of the article acknowledging the assistance of the supervisor.

There is in addition the ethical issue of the exercise of undue influence by the supervisor. In this case, it appears that the supervisor *asked* if her name could be included. As the initiative came from the supervisor, it is rather difficult to separate the act of the request from the position of authority and influence in which supervisors inevitably find themselves. Just as we consider it appropriate that research students try to follow all of the reasonable advice of their supervisors, it also behoves supervisors not to make requests on the basis of their role, rather than on the basis of reasonable argument. The relationship between supervisor and research student is inevitably a complex one, and there are responsibilities incumbent on both parties. It seems only fair to assume, however, that those responsibilities should be exercised on the basis of ethical principles, rather than upon the basis of differential power relationships.

Researchers have a general responsibility towards the academic community, and in particular to ensure that the community of academics is one which remains open both to new ideas and to unfashionable ones. Academic ideas and schools of thought do not remain popular in perpetuity. They are fashionable for a time, and then to some extent fall out of fashion. Nowhere is this more true than in research methodology. There was a time when a great deal of the research in education and the social sciences was quantitative in nature. Fashions changed with an increasing interest in qualitative and interpretative approaches. Even within the broad qualitative approach, ethnography may be popular for a time, followed perhaps by a strong interest in action research. The cyclical nature of fashions in research does raise questions about the qualities of tolerance and openness in the research community.

Some researchers have their favourite methodologies. One expects researchers to have their own specialized fields of inquiry, and it is reasonable that they should specialize in the use of specific methodologies. It may be reasonable, though, to expect a researcher who specializes in say ethnomethodology also to have a passing acquaintance with quantitative approaches. Alternatively, the statistician should have a broad understanding of the principles of say interactionism. If this is not so, within the research community there are likely to be two undesirable results. First, researchers within the different disciplines will be hampered in their communications with each other. There is the danger that they will become so enclosed within the parameters and conceptual framework of their chosen methodology that they communicate only with researchers of like mind. It would not take long for the research community to become fragmented. Second, a lack of understanding of other approaches may lead to the assumption that their own perspective is the only valid one. When a research question is being analysed initially, with a view to designing an investigation, then researchers may consider only their own approach. They will simply not be equipped in terms of expertise to design another type of research project. Such a view may sometimes lead gradually to an intolerance for other perspectives, and finally to outright criticism. In this case, the community of researchers, which should be so open to fresh ideas, may tend to operate as separate groups each working within its own paradigm.

In fact, for any particular research question, there are usually several approaches and methodologies which may be used to shed light on that question. Imagine, for example, that a high school is interested in examining its policy towards the provision of physical education and sport. One researcher may advise the school that they would be best advised to devise a questionnaire and distribute it to all students, teachers and parents, in order to gain an overview of current opinion. A different researcher may suggest that this type of approach could yield rather superficial data, and that the school would be better advised to conduct in-depth interviews with a small group of students. Researchers often have different views about the most appropriate method to use. Let us digress briefly, and examine the perspective of relativism (see Box 1.8).

Box 1.8   Theoretical perspective: relativism

Relativism is the term used to describe the situation where different groups of people have different belief systems. In the area of ethics it may refer to social groups possessing different ethical norms and values. In the area of epistemology, it may refer to two groups differing in the methods they use to establish what they regard as valid knowledge. It should be noted that there are different types of relativism. The term may be used in situations where the intent is simply to describe differences in belief systems. On the other hand it may be used in situations where different belief systems are being evaluated (see Mackie 1977: 36).

In terms of this discussion of relativism, let us explore several possible scenarios involving two groups of researchers, A and B, who each have different views about research methodology.

- *Scenario 1*
  Researchers in Group A have their favoured research methodology. They acknowledge that the favoured method of Group B is not in error, but they definitely prefer their own approach, and always use it. In addition, when their opinion is sought, they always recommend it to other researchers. Group B feel exactly the same about their favoured method.
- *Scenario 2*
  Group B has its favoured research approach. It knows very little of the method of Group A, and always uses and advocates its own approach. It feels that the method of Group A is mistaken and does not yield valid knowledge. The members of Group A have a similar approach.
- *Scenario 3*
  Group A and Group B have their own methodologies which they each feel more competent in using. However, they fully acknowledge the validity of the methodology of the other group. Both groups share the view that the research methodology which should be selected for a particular project should depend not upon the personal feelings of the researcher, but upon a rational analysis of the research question and aims. In other words, for a particular research question expressed in a particular way, there is likely to be a research approach which, other things being equal, will be more suitable than others.

We have examined these three scenarios in order to explore what we mean when we suggest that researchers have a responsibility to try to create an 'open' academic community. In the first two scenarios, both groups of researchers have acquired a form of ideological commitment to a specific methodology. The problem with this is that it may tend to close their eyes to other possibilities in research, and that their choice of methodology does not appear to depend upon the application of reason. In the third scenario, the choice of methodology is driven by a rational analysis of the research problem, and the reasons for choice may be subjected to a critical scrutiny. This is a much more open form of decision-making, and the argument would be that researchers in all types of situations have a responsibility to work towards creating this type of research community, rather than any other.

Areas of research which raise ethical issues

On a general level, the kinds of ethical issues raised by the research process involving human beings are no different from the ethical issues raised by any interactive situation with human beings. All such situations demand that other human beings should be treated with respect, should not be harmed in any way, and should be fully informed about what is being done with them. Many of these general ethical principles can be applied to a research context, but there are more specific situations which illustrate the importance of ethics. Before commencing the systematic exploration of all of these issues, it may be useful to provide a brief indication of some areas where ethical issues may, in different ways, be of critical importance.

There are, first of all, a range of situations where the participants in the research project may not be in a position to understand fully the implications of the research. The respondents could be young children, for example, who while perfectly able to provide research data, may not be old enough to appreciate the details of the research process. In such a case, there may need to be detailed discussions with parents, teachers and any other relevant adults, about what measures should be in operation in order to protect the interests of the children. The particular measures may depend upon the age of the children and the specific research context. It may not be possible to identify a standard range of procedures here, but rather to accept that each research situation involving children should be treated as an individual case.

People who are deceased may not normally be thought of as research respondents, yet they may have left extensive life-history traces, which are valuable to researchers. Examples include statistical data retained by official organizations, artefacts which they have made during their lives, notebooks and diaries, and importantly, the memories which living people have retained of them. Deceased people are clearly not in a position to give their informed consent, which places an important responsibility upon researchers to be as balanced and objective as possible in any interpretation of their lives and achievements. Important issues here include whether the deceased person should be named in any research report, and also the impact which the research may have on living relatives.

There may be research situations where adult participants, for a variety of reasons, may not understand the nature of the research process, and hence cannot consent to their participation in the research from a position of understanding. Such situations may involve adults who have had relatively little formal academic education, or participants who have a different mother tongue from the researchers; although they may have second language competence, it may be insufficient to help them understand the research context. Clearly such situations do not remove the responsibility from the researcher to ensure that all participants fully understand the programme of research before taking part.

It is not always easy to identify people who are willing to act as participants in a research project, and on occasion researchers may feel that it is necessary to provide material benefit to encourage people to take part. There are perhaps two main situations where material benefits may be offered. First, there is the situation where inducements such as small prizes may be offered to encourage people to complete and submit questionnaires. Second, participants may be offered payment which reimburses them for either expense or effort incurred in participating in the research. For example, participants may have travelling expenses refunded, be given a lunch allowance, or paid a reasonable fee to compensate them for the time taken in providing data.

Some researchers may feel that ideally the relationship between the researcher and participant should not involve any form of material benefit. The argument may be that the inducement or compensation can change the relationship and perhaps distort the way in which data are provided. Therein lies the ethical issue. If the purpose of the research is to explore impartially a subject of important social concern, the introduction of material benfits may make that the principal interest of potential participants, rather than the wish to assist in socially constructive research. It could be argued that it is better to have a smaller number of participants who are committed to the research for its own sake, rather than a greater number who are preoccupied with the benefits which they hope to acquire. However, it could also be argued that giving up one's time to take part in research is no different from giving up one's time to work at anything else. It is only reasonable to expect to be paid. Indeed, one could argue that the introduction of the principle of payment could engender a more professional approach to the providing of data.

Finally, ethical debates can arise in research situations where both parties agree about the ethical question and its importance, but disagree about the action which should be taken. The question of the intrusion into personal privacy is a case in point. Within social science research, there is a tradition of seeking to distinguish between 'private space' and 'public space'. When potential research participants are in their private space, researchers may not normally be justified in keeping field notes of their actions, without abiding by the principles of informed consent. On the other hand, if potential participants are within a public space, then the same conventions need not apply. Of course, trying to distinguish between private and public spaces may be highly problematic. In the discussion in Box 1.9, two researchers explore the different types of situations in which they might feel justified in keeping field notes of conversations or dialogue.

Box 1.9   Ethical dialogue: keeping field notes

A: If we were having coffee in the refectory at the university, I wouldn't feel very happy making notes on a student conversation going on nearby.

B: Not even if they were talking really loudly?

A: Well, if the conversation was essentially private, and wasn't intended for me, then I would feel that I was intruding. It wouldn't really matter how loud they were talking.

B: So is the criterion whether or not you are intended to be part of the audience?

A: Well, that would be my first attempt at a criterion.

B: So, if you are part of the intended audience in some way, it is OK to keep field notes, and if you are not part of the audience, then you shouldn't?

A: That's roughly my argument.

B: What if we wanted to collect data on dialogue at say a cricket ground then? We are sitting on the terraces and there are all the usual comments flying around. Could we keep field notes?

A: Well perhaps! If there were a parent and child sitting next to me, and having a private conversation, I don't think I would want to keep notes even if I could hear. On the other hand, if there were groups of people shouting out jokes and remarks, I think I would feel part of the audience for that, so I think it would be reasonable to keep notes.

B: But using your criterion would require interpreting whether remarks were being made privately, or being directed to a general audience of which you would be part?

A: I agree, the distinction is not always very clear.

Researcher A has succeeded in developing a general principle as a guide. However, it is almost the nature of ethics that it is often easier to think of an exception to a principle than to develop a principle in the first place! In this case, we could imagine situations where we are part of an audience, and yet may feel that it was inappropriate to keep field notes without asking for permission. A consultation in a doctor's surgery is one example, as is a discussion at a school parents' evening. The issues raised by privacy in research are thus very complex, but this has been a brief attempt to map out some of the ethical territory involved. (For a discussion of issues of privacy in research, see Bryman 2001: 483.)

Well, I have tried in this chapter to sketch some broad areas of research ethics, and to illustrate the complexity of the issues involved. Now it is time to get down to the basic questions of designing a research project and collecting data. The next three chapters look at ethical questions which can arise during the research process, from the design phase, through the data-collection phase, and in the analysis and dissemination of the results. These are the practical matters which affect you as a researcher, so let us start with the issue of identifying respondents.

2 Research and the respondent

Ethical issues before the research commences

Procedures for identifying and recruiting potential respondents

It is easy to imagine that research is a completely sequential process, which involves one stage leading logically on to the next, and so on. Life would be a lot simpler if that were the case! In fact, research is much more likely to be an activity in which we have to consider many diverse issues simultaneously. There is an important logical thought process involved in research, but the different components of that process do not usually line themselves up in a nice neat sequence. We often have to deal with problems in research when they arise, and some issues, such as ethics, arise at different stages of the research process.

The identification of respondents is a case in point. We do not usually select our research participants in isolation from all our other thoughts about the research project. We think about our research aims and the research questions which they raise; we consider the overall research design and the data-collection strategies which we might employ; and we reflect on our study population, sampling strategy and the people who we might approach to provide data. We often have all of these matters circulating around in our mind at the same time; ethical questions are an important aspect of these deliberations. We might, for example, have developed a sophisticated research design and sampling procedure, but on reflection we may realize that the selection of participants raises serious ethical difficulties. (For aspects of contacting participants, see Creswell 1998.)

Let us suppose that you plan to investigate the role of decision-making in committee meetings in a large organization. Quite possibly you spend a considerable amount of your working time in meetings, and are intrigued by the way in which decisions either evolve or are taken. You decide to take copious notes during a variety of meetings, recording verbal exchanges and the discussions which lead up to decision-taking. You decide not to inform anyone, since you reason that what you are doing is little different from the taking of minutes. In any case, you feel that once respondents knew they were being observed, the entire character of the meeting would change. However, after some reflection on the methodology, you come to the conclusion that there is a distinction between taking minutes of a meeting and note-taking of the kind you have planned. In the former case, all members of the meeting know there is the possibility that what they say may be recorded. They may not agree with the record of the minutes, but at least at the next meeting they have an opportunity to challenge the record. However, when note-taking is covert, the fact that it is done in secret eliminates the possibility of challenging the accuracy of the record. The purpose of this example is to demonstrate that a consideration of ethical issues should ideally be integrated with all phases of the research design process. If this is done then you can feel more confident that your research process is fair to the people involved.

Some research methodologies have an inherent means of allowing respondents to select themselves. If you are using self-completion question-naires in survey research, you will be very fortunate to have a 100 per cent response rate. Some people will reply and others will choose not to return their questionnaires. There is nothing unreasonable about the exercise of individual free will and autonomy in this way, and there is no reason why some people should choose not to participate in a research programme. The only assump-tion in this is that all potential respondents, whether they choose to take part or not, should be fully informed about all relevant aspects of the research. We will explore this particular issue in the next section of the chapter.

People who are sent a questionnaire are usually able to sit in their own homes, and take a calm decision about whether to complete it and put it in the post. However, researchers sometimes approach people in person to ask if they would be prepared to provide data. There is nothing wrong with this in principle, but we ought to be aware that it may not give people sufficient time to make a considered decision. Potential research participants may find it difficult to refuse a request. They may prefer not to take part, but cannot think of a suitable reason to give. They may not really want to be interviewed about the research topic, but on the other hand do not want to appear unhelpful. If they are known to you, for example friends or colleagues, they may feel obliged to help with the research, even though they would prefer to decline your invitation. There is also the issue that unwilling participants may not be truly helpful for the research programme which you have in mind. It would be far better to have people who are interested and willing to take part. From a procedural point of view, the key issue is that people should be given sufficient time to make up their mind.

There is no absolutely correct procedure in these situations, but one idea is to contact all potential respondents by phone or letter, and explain the main aspects of the research. You can express your hope that they will take part, and say that you will contact them again in a few days' time, to ask if they will definitely be respondents. Alternatively, you could enclose a reply slip and pre-paid envelope with the letter. Email offers the same possibility for giving people a period of thought. Some people may decide not to take part, but at least you will know that those who do accept your offer have thought about the research, and taken a positive decision to help.

The principle of informed consent

A central feature of social science research ethics is the principle that par-ticipants should be fully informed about a research project before they assent to taking part. This principle is usually known as informed consent. It may immediately occur to us that this idea begs the question of what 'fully informed' actually means in practice. There would potentially be an almost unlimited amount of information that could be passed on to possible respondents. In practical terms we would have to stop somewhere. As a broad definition of 'fully informed', we might say that it should include any information which a participant might conceivably need in order to make a decision about whether or not to participate. We will need to look later at specific instances of this issue.

The notion of informed consent seems to be related to a number of com-monly held ethical principles. It seems to contravene ideas of fairness to expect people to take a decision when they are not in possession of the relevant 'facts'. We also speak of people having a 'right to know' and a right to information. Whereas we cannot reasonably claim that people should have access to all possible knowledge in the world, we may feel that a right exists to information which may have a direct bearing upon ourselves as an individual. There is also the question of our personal autonomy. We may feel that our autonomy to take a decision and then act upon that decision is severely constrained if we do not have access to relevant data.

A difficulty may arise in situations where the researcher is sensitive to the issue of informed consent, but has difficulty explaining the technical aspects of the research to participants. Perhaps the language used is too esoteric and specialized, or perhaps the researcher is not skilled at presenting academic ideas in a readily understandable manner. However, the principle of informed consent should not be diluted. A way should be found to explain the basics of the research project to the participants, in a manner which they can under-stand. Any simplification of ideas should not be so excessive as to distort the ideas themselves.

The principle of informed consent applies not only to all situations with human participants, but also to research on social groups and organizations, businesses and corporate entities. These may range from schools, to local government departments, to small companies or multinational corporations. Although such organizations may sometimes appear to act as impersonal entities, they are composed of human beings and merit the application of informed consent. (For a discussion on informed consent, see Burns 2000: 18.)

There may be difficulties with informed consent in situations where participants are part of a hierarchical work structure. They may need reassuring about the parameters of issues on which their organization would approve of their commenting. This may necessitate the researcher engaging in preliminary discussions with the organization, before approaching potential participants. Let us look at how this problem might occur in practice. In Box 2.1 the discussion is taking place between two researchers who are planning some research on management styles in an organization.

Box 2.1 Ethical dialogue: informed consent in an organizational context

A: What we are really trying to uncover here are the private views of people in the offices on the management style of the organization.

B: OK, but they will never talk to us, I mean really talk to us, unless they feel absolutely empowered to do so, and also that confidentiality is absolutely assured.

A: Well, we can deal with confidentiality. If we explain our systems for handling data, hopefully that will be sufficient reassurance. But we also need something to filter down from senior management, saying that people can participate.

B: Right, we basically need an email to all staff from the chief executive, saying that she has commissioned our research, and would like people to be involved.

A: And she could also say that she has asked us to ensure the anonymity of all participants. Oh, and we really want some sort of statement that staff are encouraged to discuss with us any management issues which we raise in the interviews.

B: I don't think there will be a problem with this.

A: Nor do I. Once this email has gone round, we should be able to ask people to take part, and get a reasonable response.

The researchers are rightly sensitive to the feelings of the workers in the organization. The workers will understandably be cautious about making comments on the management style of the organization, unless they are confident that the management at the highest level approves of their involvement. Even then, respondents will almost certainly want there to be a system which ensures that comments cannot be traced back to their originator. Such a system may have to ensure that data cannot be identified with even a specific department.

Reassurances on the existence of such systems are a necessary part of the information which potential respondents legitimately need. In order to make an informed decision about participation, they do need to understand the attitude of the organization's management towards this research. This would be important for most kinds of research in an organization, but is clearly significant when the topic of research is the style of the management within the organization.

Research participants may be concerned that there could be adverse repercussions for them, if they made comments which were critical of the management style. Informed consent becomes particularly significant where there is the possibility, however remote, of adverse consequences for a participant.

Written information on the research project, and obtaining written consent

One of the slightly complicated issues with informed consent is deciding the limits of the information to be passed on to potential respondents. There is likely to be so much information that could be provided, that the researcher inevitably has to be selective. Potential respondents may be particularly interested in those features of the research which might have significant consequences for them. Arguably it is the responsibility of the researcher to try to anticipate as many issues as possible, which might result in such consequences. However, this does pose slight moral questions.

Researchers may take the view that all they can reasonably be expected to do is to lay the basic facts of the research before the potential respondents and leave them to form a judgement. This assumes that the respondent is able to anticipate any problematic consequences which might arise. The alternative view is for the researcher to anticipate any difficulties wherever possible, and to make these clear to potential respondents. All respondents are different, and some aspects of the research may affect some respondents and not others. You may feel as a researcher that it is unfair that you should be expected to anticipate possible problems which might occur for a respondent. However, many researchers have an appreciation of the kinds of difficulties which can arise for respondents, and it does not seem too unreasonable to expect them to explain these in at least general terms.

The next issue which arises is the manner in which the selected information is to be passed on to respondents. The most natural way is simply to tell respondents, using brief notes as a reminder of the key issues to be mentioned. The problem here is that even with the use of a prompt card, there may be major inconsistencies in what is said to different people. Respondents may ask questions and this may cause you to digress in your account. One strategy is to prepare a card or flyer which describes the key aspects of the research, and to distribute these to all potential respondents. The advantage of this is that at least all respondents receive the standard information. This may well be supplemented by oral discussion and conversation, but at least you can feel reassured that a core of information about the research has been disseminated.

This leads on to a slightly more problematic area, and that is the mechanism which is used to establish that the respondent actually consents to participate in the research. The two alternatives would appear to be a simple oral agreement or a written agreement. However, it may be that an undue emphasis upon technical agreements may move the entire research process away from a voluntary, cooperative ethos, perhaps to the detriment of the research. Perhaps what is more important is to ensure that the core information, provided to all potential respondents, contains an accurate summary of the contribution required of the participant, and stresses that the participant may withdraw from the research process at any time on request. As an additional safeguard, participants could be promised that any data provided by them will be returned to them on request.

Such arrangements tend to create much more of a cooperative relationship between the researcher and the participant. The researcher begins by informing the participant to the best of their ability about the proposed research, and inviting the participant to provide data. If the participant agrees to help, it is on the understanding that should the situation prove to be uncongenial in any way, then the participant can withdraw. Not only that, but also the participant is regarded as the owner of the data which they have provided, and hence may reclaim that data should it be felt necessary to withdraw from the research. The relationship between researcher and participant should be a mature one, in which both parties try to be sensitive to the possible concerns of the other.

Potential disadvantage or harm which might affect respondents

It is part of the informed consent process that the researcher should try to anticipate any undesirable consequences for the potential participant. In medical research and the field trial of new medications, there are clearly potentially serious consequences to be considered. In the social science area, the nature of potentially adverse consequences can be more difficult to predict.

For example, you might be collecting oral history data on employment in your local town, and you interview local residents. In the middle of one interview the interviewee suddenly bursts into tears. It transpires that he was thinking about his early childhood and the relative who looked after him when his father was in the armed forces. As a researcher you would naturally feel sorry that the interviewee was upset, and would hope that you had done everything reasonable to avoid such an outcome. It might be reasonable to point out to potential interviewees that reliving the past can sometimes be an emotional experience. However, not everyone will react in this way, and predicting discomfort or distress during the data-gathering process may be impossible.

Adverse consequences for respondents can include psychological effects, of the type just described. There may be personal consequences which result primarily from the public disclosure of remarks which should not have been attributed to a named individual. In some cases, particularly with surveys or large-scale studies, there may conceivably be consequences for larger groups of people or for whole communities. Let us look briefly at each of these in turn.

Social science research may often deal with matters which are deceptively ordinary, such as the family, relationships at work, and the ways in which people spend their leisure time. Nevertheless, these are often areas about which people may have strong feelings. If we start to talk to someone about relationships at work, it is a fair assumption that before long we will touch a raw nerve, and raise emotive issues. We may easily stray into areas which the interviewee or respondent would prefer to avoid. They may continue with the process of providing data or they may take up the option to withdraw. Either way, we may have inadvertently caused some distress. On the other hand, if as researchers we always avoided any issue which could remotely be sensitive to someone, then we would risk making our research so bland that it would not generate any useful data. In the case of interviews, it is probably worth making it clear to respondents that they can decline to answer a question, or decline to discuss a particular topic. Another possible strategy is that, as an interview develops, the interviewer provides advance warning of questions on a particular topic. The interviewee may then be invited to reflect upon whether they wish to answer questions on that subject.

The question of confidentiality will be raised several times in this book, and in detail in Chapter 5. In this particular context, it is important for researchers to remember that respondents may often say something during a research interview, which they would not have said in a different context. It could be something about employers, friends or relatives. No matter how many reassurances they have received from the researcher about anonymity, and the use of fictional names in any research report, they may still have residual concerns about either what they have said, or the particular way in which they have expressed themselves. A simple strategy which can be used to set their minds at rest is to ask them if they would like, on reflection, to rephrase anything they have said. They can be offered this opportunity either several times during the interview, or at the end. This is not an invitation to interviewees to keep changing their minds, but rather to invite them to re-express their ideas or to state things a little more precisely. This enables them to pause and to reconsider, and perhaps to redirect the emphasis of what they have said. This should help to remove any residual concerns they have.

When research is to be conducted in a large organization or among a local community, the actual research process will inevitably have some effect upon the people present. Almost certainly there will be some change to what we might term the social ecology. Imagine for example, a team of university researchers conducting a study of a large comprehensive school, which involved interviewing staff and students. There would be a lot of discussion among the students about the unfamiliar people around the school, and conjecture about the purpose of the visit. The researchers would probably try to disrupt the school as little as possible, but nevertheless, their period in the school would have some sort of impact. No doubt, the headteacher would have taken this into account before giving permission for the research to go ahead. Sometimes social science researchers conduct field research in the general community, rather than in a specific institution, and here also there can arise the issue of disruption to the social ecology. Consider the situation described in Box 2.2.

Box 2.2   Ethical dilemma: potential impact of field research

---

You are planning to conduct research in a community consisting of different ethnic groups in which there has been a history of significant community harmony and integration between the various groups. You wish to explore possible reasons for the harmonious relationships which have developed. You are aware that in one or two neighbouring towns, there has been noticeable conflict between different ethnic groups.

In preparation for your research, you inform local community leaders and brief them on the plans for the field research. Although they are not completely antagonistic to the idea, they express concerns that the actual process of researching relations between ethnic groups may heighten differences with which people are not currently concerned. They suggest that race and ethnicity are not significant issues in the community at the moment, but by drawing attention to them, they may become so. You and your co-researchers pause to reflect on this.

This is a dilemma for the researchers. There is no way of knowing whether the community leaders are right. They are not saying that the research will certainly have a disruptive effect on the community. However, they have outlined one possible result of the research, and it is a consequence that the researchers would clearly wish to avoid. The researchers have also become conscious that if at any time in the future, there were problems with community harmony, then this might be blamed on the research. The logical alternatives would seem to be to ignore the possibility, to abandon the research altogether, or to adapt the research design in order to minimize the risk outlined by the community leaders.

Now that the issue has been raised, it would seem imprudent not to consider it in some way. On the other hand, to abandon the research could be an overreaction to a problem which might never arise. A compromise would be to review the sampling procedure for the research, in order to cause as little disruption to the community as possible. If a large number of respondents were chosen, distributed throughout the community, then many people would hear of the research project. This may be the situation which was concerning the community leaders. On the other hand, if a more restricted sample were chosen, and the purpose of the research carefully explained, the impact of the research could be reduced. This may not be perfect in terms of research design, but it could go some way towards assuaging the fears of the community leaders. The latter could also be consulted in the selection of respondents. In purely research terms, this may result in a loss of objectivity, but compensation could be made in the analysis of data, and it may be viewed as a compromise worth making in the circumstances.

Will respondents be likely to gain in any way from participation in the research?

It is always worthwhile considering if there are ways in which your respondents may gain anything from taking part in the research. After all, we as researchers are the ones who are asking a favour of respondents. We are asking them to give up their time and to help us. It is not usually essential for the research that the respondents gain something tangible from it, but we may be able to structure the research process in such a way that respondents both enjoy it and find it interesting.

It is sometimes easy to forget that it is we as researchers who often stand to gain a great deal from the research activity. We may want to use the research in order to gain a new qualification such as a research degree; we may intend to write up the data and results as an article in an academic journal; or we may want the data to disseminate to colleagues or to help us to write a book. These kinds of goals may also have the secondary advantage of helping us to further our careers. But what of the respondents?

They will probably not be able to look forward to any tangible benefits such as these. Nevertheless, there is no reason why the process should not be fulfilling for them in different ways. They may find it interesting simply to be involved in a research project. They may have no previous experience of social science research, and may enjoy watching the way researchers approach the data-collection process. Quite apart from any responsibility which we may have in relation to informed consent, it can make the process of participation more interesting if respondents understand the background to the research. They might like to know the numbers of other people who are receiving questionnaires or being interviewed. They might find it interesting to know about the original idea for the research, or the use to which the final results will be put. Although knowing these things may not necessarily result in the respondents providing data which are any different from that which they would otherwise have provided, it should at least enable them to appreciate more the relevance of the research.

Respondents are in many ways at the centre of the research process. It is their opinions and comments which will form the basis of our analysis. It is their views that matter. Once we have designed the research in a certain way and decided upon our sample, then we have committed ourselves to collecting data from our chosen respondents. They hence become important people to us, and it is worth making sure that they understand how much we appreciate and value their views. The respondents may not have too many tangible benefits from the process, but they should feel valued. The research process can help respondents to have an enhanced sense of their own worth. As they realize that they are at the focus of the research process, and that the researchers are really interested in their opinions, this can result in a heightened feeling of self-esteem.

In relation to this issue, there may sometimes be a benefit to be gained from interview research in particular, whereby the respondent is actually encouraged and helped to clarify their own ideas on an issue. This can happen when we are simply filling in a questionnaire. The very act of thinking carefully about our response can help to cystallize our thoughts on a matter. When we are conducting a research interview, we should bear in mind that the interviewee may have been in the process of developing ideas on a particular issue, but may have an understandable difficulty in giving expression to complex issues. If, as researchers, we can help respondents to clarify their ideas, this is a tangible contribution. Having said this, however, it is necessary to exercise caution in case the researcher asks leading questions, or in other ways inadvertently encourages the respondent towards a particular viewpoint.

Researching vulnerable groups of people

Before we start to examine the research ethics issues here, let us define those people who we consider to be vulnerable in research terms. Broadly speaking they are those individuals or categories of people who may not have the required degree of understanding (for whatever reason) to give their informed consent to participation in research. A fairly obvious category is that of children. Depending upon their age, they may not be able to understand the implications of what is being asked of them. There are a number of other categories of potential respondents who may be vulnerable. People whose first language is different from that of the researcher may simply not be able to understand everything that is being said to them. In some situations, such as those involving employment, the researcher may be higher in the hierarchical system than participants, who may feel pressurized to help with the research even though they would prefer not to participate. This may be the case even when the researcher does nothing to encourage such a feeling of pressure. The feeling derives entirely from the existence of a hierarchical relationship.

Other groups of people for a variety of reasons are socially or economically vulnerable, such as unemployed or homeless people. They may feel uncertain, lacking in confidence, anxious or preoccupied with a solution to their social situation. In this frame of mind they may not react in the manner in which they would normally react, to a request to take part in research. In an analogous situation, people who are suffering ill-health may be so concerned about this that it affects their response to a request from a researcher.

Some individuals or groups may, through limitations of education, have difficulty in understanding what is being requested of them. It may be difficult to predict when this might be the case, and the researcher should be conscious of the dangers of making assumptions about specific categories of people. Some elderly people may not understand all of the implications of research requests, but this will not apply by any means to all elderly people.

The question of vulnerability in research terms is a complicated issue. On the one hand, as researchers we need to be sensitive to the situation of those people who we feel may not understand the implications of requests to participate. Either we need to help them to understand, or we need to take advice as to whether it is ethical to continue with the research. On the other hand, we do not want to be condescending towards people, or to make unwarranted assumptions about their competence, or to engage in a process of social labelling. There is, as with most ethical situations, a fine line to draw.

Let us look first at some general strategies which can be adopted, and then examine a specific case study and the way in which we might respond to that. One of the most useful general approaches in these kinds of situations is to submit your research plans for consideration by your peers. If there are any doubts that the respondents may not be able to understand completely the research project, you can take the views of other researchers as to whether they think the research is still in principle ethically defensible. It is often reassuring in these circumstances, if your peers are formally organized into something such as an ethics committee, whose records are minuted. They may take the view that in the absence of full informed consent, the research should be abandoned, or they may suggest some short-term strategies which can help ensure that the respondents are fully informed before consent is obtained. Finally, they may suggest that it is not feasible to obtain informed consent from respondents, but that it would be ethically acceptable to obtain consent from an appropriate third party.

In the case of respondents whose first language is different from that of the researcher, a translator or interpreter may be helpful. If respondents are having difficulty with the style of English used to describe the research, then peers may suggest useful ways in which the description can be either simplified or made more relevant. In either case it is important that the description is not so diluted that the essence of the information is lost.

The strategy of obtaining third party consent may be relevant where school pupils are to be research participants. While it may be feasible to explain the research in outline to the children, the fully informed consent would be obtained from parents or guardians, teachers or other relevant professionals. If this strategy is suggested after careful peer review, consideration must be given to defining those professionals who should be involved in the consent process. An ethics committee may advise on this. Where third party consent is sought, it is preferable to obtain the consent in writing.

Another broad principle when anticipating research with potentially vulnerable people is to regard ethical decision-making as a gradual process; one does not try to reach a full and final decision about an entire research project, but proceeds incrementally, reaching decisions about small aspects of the research. One could proceed with a small pilot study, for example, in order to try to judge any effects of the research on the respondents. If this were combined with peer review at each stage, it would go a long way to providing adequate safeguards. The conceptual position is that decision-making in relation to ethical issues is often so complex that a number of different questions have to be carefully weighed. This process sometimes has to take place over a protracted period, as one gradually works one's way towards a consensus.

Let us now examine a case study involving a potentially vulnerable group, and then reflect on how a theoretical perspective may help us resolve the dilemma. Consider the case of a sociologist who would like to investigate the health problems of older homeless men and women who are leading an itinerant life. The sociologist is concerned that as a group they may have a wide range of health problems, some of which could be treated fairly easily and that this would improve their quality of life. The sociologist hopes to use the research to publicize the health needs of such people, and to encourage the relevant health authorities to establish an improved programme of regular intervention. Some colleagues draw the attention of the sociologist to the possibility that some of the homeless people may be antagonistic to the idea of help from statutory bodies. They may feel that even the research process is a threat to their independence and the freedom of their way of life. Several preliminary interviews conducted by the sociologist suggest that there is a possibility that regular medical checks may have a restricting influence upon the lifestyle of the research respondents.

The sociologist is thus experiencing something of a dilemma, by wanting to provide better health care for the homeless people, but equally not wishing to disturb the social ecology of their lifestyle. When we are faced with ethical dilemmas, either in a research context or in daily life, we can sometimes seek help from a general ethical rule of the type proposed by Kant. Alternatively, we can try to explore the consequences of the possible actions and select the action which is likely to bring about the greatest good. We may feel that in the case of research ethics, some dilemmas are so complex that neither of these strategies will offer a way to find a solution. Let us consider the analysis of the philosopher W.D. Ross (see Box 2.3).

Box 2.3   Theoretical perspective: prima facie duties

W.D. Ross felt that in life human beings had a number of important ethical responsibilities. These could not be thought of as absolute responsibilities, but were nevertheless very important. Ross termed these prima facie duties, and included among them the duty to try to improve the well-being of other people, and also the duty of not harming others. Sometimes, Ross felt, one duty might suggest a particular course of action, while a different prima facie duty would point to doing something else. The final decision would depend to a great extent upon the context of the particular dilemma. After weighing up the relevant duties, it might be decided that in one particular case, duty X was more significant than duty Y (see Hudson 1970: 95).

Perhaps Ross's type of analysis offers the sociologist a way forward. The context of this dilemma is certainly important. The homeless people are a vulnerable group, both in research terms and in other ways. They are not living in the mainstream of society and cannot be expected to predict all of the possible consequences of the research. On the one hand, the researcher is very well motivated and wishes to help them. The sociologist has a prima facie duty to try to provide more regular and institutionalized health care, but is conscious of a responsibility not to disturb their lifestyle. This may have unanticipated, adverse consequences. Thus the two duties are in conflict. The sociologist might conclude that while it is important to help people, there is the risk of an unpredictable level of harm. There is nothing to stop the people accessing health care on an ad-hoc basis, according to need, and this will not be likely to undermine their lifestyle. It may be decided that the research is inappropriate, and that the sociologist may be better advised to research ways in which the health authorities are able to respond, if requested by homeless people.

Obtaining access to the research field via 'gatekeepers'

The term 'gatekeeper' is often used to describe the person who controls access to a location where it is hoped to carry out research. The term is typically used in a metaphorical sense to suggest individuals who have management or administrative control in an organization, and who can decide in absolute terms whether you be permitted to carry out your research. The managing director of a company, the principal of a college and the headteacher in a school are examples of gatekeepers in this sense.

Now one might be forgiven for thinking that the relationship between researcher and gatekeeper is likely to be one of conflict. The researcher might be perceived as someone who wants to carry out the research at all costs, while the gatekeeper might be seen as fundamentally concerned with protecting the institution, and tending to apply stringent conditions to any research process. There is no reason at all, however, for these aims to be in opposition to each other. What is fundamentally required is that researcher and gatekeeper should make a serious attempt to see the point of view of the other; that is why this is, at least partly, an ethical situation.

The relationship between researcher and gatekeeper can be fully symbiotic. They both have a great deal to gain from the relationship, although it could be argued that the gatekeeper potentially has more to lose: the researcher can always move on to another research field, whereas the gatekeeper may have to reduce the impact of insensitive research practice. Nevertheless, many people in positions of authority in organizations would often like to have research conducted on aspects of their work. Headteachers might be interested in a systematic study of the attitudes of pupils to homework, or of the impact of a new approach to monitoring student progress. It is true that the research project proposed to a gatekeeper may not ideally be the one that would be chosen, but nevertheless, it may be possible to compromise with the researcher and create a research programme which would at least partially be of use to the school.

No matter how interesting or potentially useful the research, gatekeepers will inevitably have concerns about the impact of the research on the organization. They will be concerned lest the normal day-to-day functioning of the organization be disturbed, or that some confidential information may be disclosed outside the organization. The researcher thus has an ethical obligation to fully inform the gatekeeper about the proposed research, particularly in relation to any features which might affect the gatekeeper's decision. It may help the researcher's case if they can demonstrate an awareness of areas where the research may have an impact upon the organization. This may reassure the gatekeeper that the research process will not have an adverse effect on the work of the organization.

The researcher should indicate the anticipated parameters of the research. It is difficult for a researcher to predict exactly from whom data will be collected and under what circumstances. The researcher will not want to have to get separate permission every time there is a slight change to the research design. It is sensible at this stage to outline as honestly as possible the main research plan, and then to indicate possible directions in which the research might develop. If an overall approval can be gained, it will provide the researcher with a certain freedom of action. If the gatekeeper has some residual concerns, it would be a good idea for the researcher to agree a straightforward procedure for obtaining new permission if required.

The role of ethics committees and boards

An ethics committee is a formal committee established by an organization or institution, to monitor ethical issues in research programmes. Ethics committees can be set up to consider any other issues besides research, but we are here concerned with those with a brief to consider research. In the broadest terms, ethics committees have two main areas of activity. First, they are involved in the development and dissemination of good practice in research ethics. In this capacity, they may decide to develop a code of practice for research students, researchers and lecturers, in relation to ethical issues in research design and implementation. Second, they are involved in the peer review of research designs and proposals, to ensure that they address relevant ethical issues. In this capacity an ethics committee is usually empowered by a senior authority in an organization, to take and implement decisions within its remit. To this end, an ethics committee must be able not only to arrive at decisions, but also to act on and enforce its decisions. It is concerned not only with the establishment of standards of ethical research, but also with ensuring that researchers comply with those standards.

Many researchers come across ethics committees when they submit their research proposals for approval. The main approval committee may subsume the functions of an ethics committee, or there may be a separate committee for ethics issues. Ethics committees are sometimes perceived by researchers as a hurdle in the sometimes lengthy process of gaining approval for a research project. In fact, quite apart from the intrinsic value of the help and advice which they offer, they provide a sense of organizational support for what you are doing. If you are a research student, for example, and are applying to start doctoral research, then the fact of your proposal having been vetted by a university ethics committee provides reassurance about the ethics of your research design. You will have more confidence in embarking on your research, knowing that it meets current accepted standards. Unanticipated difficulties can arise, but at least you have the confidence that your research design has been approved by experienced researchers.

When you are talking to gatekeepers and others in the research field, it is helpful to be able to say that your research has been approved by your institutional ethics committee. It is also a form of safeguard for the participants in the research. If issues are raised by participants, it is reassuring for both you and them to be able to explain that your research has been through a vetting procedure. It will almost certainly be the norm for ethics committees to keep careful minutes of the meetings; as a researcher, it may be useful for you to keep the relevant minutes of the discussion of your research. It may be useful for reference, to check that you have complied with their requirements, and also simply as a record of the approval of your research programme. (Gatekeepers and ethics committees are discussed in Greig and Taylor 1999: 151–3.)

It is implicit in this discussion that ethics committees should have the power to veto a research programme and to refuse to grant institutional support. In practice, an ethics committee would usually make recommendations for the improvement of the research design, and the researcher would then make these amendments. In the final analysis it is important that ethics committees have the power to withhold approval.

Obtaining relevant permission to conduct research

Sometimes when a researcher is negotiating entry to the research field, limitations are put on the access to potential respondents. In some cases the researcher may feel that this is reasonable, and that it will not adversely affect the research. On the other hand, if the researcher feels that the restrictions are unjustified, and that they will distort the research, a form of ethical dilemma can arise. Essentially the researcher may be faced with a number of alternative courses of action, all of which are to varying degrees unpalatable. Let us consider a specific case study in Box 2.4 and the different ways in which it might be resolved.

The researcher is basically happy with the approach taken by the three headteachers who have allowed him access. He appreciates that there may be all kinds of reasons why some teachers would prefer him not to observe some classes, and regards this as perfectly reasonable. He has the reassurance that he can at least approach all teachers in the schools, and discuss his research interests with them.

He is unhappy about the fourth school because he feels, rightly or wrongly, that the headteacher is trying to control the research situation, and make sure that he speaks only to those teachers who are regarded as suitable by the headteacher. The researcher feels that this is an ethical issue, because a

---

Box 2.4   Ethical dilemma: restrictions on research

A research student is exploring issues concerned with the pastoral care of pupils in four high schools, along with procedures for managing situations where pupils exhibit unacceptable behaviour in class. Three of the headteachers have said that in principle the researcher can observe any class in the school, on the assumption that the class teacher and head of department are in agreement. The headteachers have pointed out that there may be special circumstances in which a class teacher may prefer an observer not to be present, and that those wishes should be respected. In general, however, the headteachers supported the research and gave the researcher access in principle to all school staff. The fourth headteacher wished to impose restrictions. He said that he was happy to support the research, but would draw up a programme of interview times for the researcher, with key staff whom he selected. Classroom observation would be possible, but with certain selected staff. The researcher was left to reflect on how to respond to this offer.

---

limited and probably distorted picture of the school will emerge, and this is completely avoidable by the open and honest collection of data. The researcher is tempted to approach individual teachers, despite the attitude of the headteacher, but decides this would not be compatible with his own ethical stance. He decides to speak to the headteacher again, and ask if he could be given wider access. The headteacher again refuses, and gives as his reason that it would be too disruptive to the normal functioning of the school. The researcher is further reinforced in his view that the head is trying to stage-manage the process.

The researcher concludes that if he wants to collect data in the school, that he will have to abide by the wishes of the headteacher. However, he feels it will be relevant and important to document the permission-seeking process in his research report, in order at least to provide a comparison with the other schools. It will also be important to indicate in his report the number of teachers in the fourth school with whom he was prevented from having a discussion. In addition, as he was known by the headteacher to be in the school as a researcher, he felt it was reasonable that he maintained a detailed field diary while he was present in the school. He intended to restrict this field diary to events he observed while simply moving about the school in the public areas such as corridors, foyers, playgrounds, the main hall and dining room. He did not intend to deliberately venture into areas which he would not normally use.

It is difficult to judge whether the researcher was ethically entitled to maintain a field diary without the explicit permission of the headteacher. One may imagine that the headteacher would give permission, but ask what would be included in the diary. Of course, the researcher could not predict this. The next step may be for the headteacher to wish to read samples from the diary before it was released. Clearly it becomes difficult to know when the seeking of permission has reached a reasonable limit. The researcher clearly took the view that having been granted entry to the school as a researcher, he was entitled to record as data anything which he routinely saw.

Reaching agreement with institutions or organizations in which research will be conducted

In the previous case the researcher may not have agreed with the response that he received from the fourth headteacher, but at least he knew who to approach. He knew the identity of the significant gatekeeper, and hence whose permission to seek. However, in some cases, researchers feel the need to ask and obtain permission to conduct research, and yet are unclear about who they should ask. Consider the case of two research students who wish to conduct a sociological field study of a town park. They are interested in treating the park as a social space or even as a type of community, and documenting the different forms of social interactions. They are concerned that as the park is owned and administered by the local authority, they should ask permission of someone, not least because their activities as social researchers might be misconstrued. They discuss how they might proceed in Box 2.5.

The ethical issue of seeking permission to approach respondents is not as clear here for a variety of reasons. Members of the public have access to the park, in a way that they do not in a school or commercial company. One clearly cannot just walk into a private building and start asking questions of people, whereas it is less obvious that this cannot be done in a park. Also, the controlling authority is a little less clear in the case of the park, compared with a school, hospital or industrial company. The local authority employees who work in the park will be part of a probably large local authority department which includes a wide range of facilities. There will possibly be a complex hierarchical management structure.

Nevertheless, the two researchers have formed the view that it is wise to seek advice, even if the consensus later appears to be that formal permission from someone is not necessary. This seems a sensible route to follow. The process of discussion may in itself solve the problem by pointing to someone whose permission should be asked. On the other hand, the consultation may simply suggest that it is reasonable to proceed with the research. At least if the two researchers are challenged in any way, they can demonstrate that they have done their best to take advice. (For the issue of obtaining permission, see Van Kammen and Stouthamer-Loeber 1998: 377.)

Box 2.5 Ethical dialogue: permission to research in publicly owned spaces

---

A: My main concern is that if we were to just walk up to someone, say we are researchers, and then ask if we can interview them, they might very well go and complain to someone. Actually, I might not blame them!

B: OK, but the park is a public space. TV interviewers go up to people on the street, and what about people in town with questionnaires? They just walk up to people. I can't really see the difference.

A: I know what you mean. For me, it's because the park is fairly quiet. People have an expectation that they can go there and be on their own. I don't think that is as true in town. People can come up to you and ask for directions, or ask the time.

B: I can see it could be awkward. On the other hand who do we ask for permission? Are the parks department really going to be interested? Perhaps we should ask at the police station.

A: We might also look a bit strange, just wandering about on our own, and stopping every now and again to ask people questions. I can see people avoiding us and walking in the opposite direction!

B: Well, one idea would be to turn it into a kind of participant observation study. We might get the parks department to give us a temporary job as a kind of cover! We could be weeding flower-beds one minute, and then writing up our field notes.

A: My main point is that I think the park is different from the high street. It might be a public space, but it is a very managed public space. People have certain expectations of it. If we are going to approach people for data I think it is only fair to think out carefully how we will approach them. I think we have to start at the parks department, and ask them for advice. They may not want to know anything about the research, but at least we have tried.

B: You've persuaded me. I think we have to at least seek advice. Then if we are challenged by anyone, at least we have done something.

It can also be argued that one of the key features of ethical decision-making is the process of discussion and consultation. This implies that people are willing to listen to others, to take advice and to recognize the complexity of ethical issues. It suggests that people realize that there is usually more than one side to an ethical issue. In research ethics, as much as elsewhere, it is essential that we take careful cognizance of the views of other people.

3 Research and the respondent
Ethical issues during the research

The ethics of recording data

It is during the data-collection phase of research that there is arguably the closest interaction between researcher and respondent. Such interaction inevitably generates situations involving ethical issues. Some of these issues can be predicted, while others arise spontaneously during the data-gathering process. One has only to think of the complex interactions which take place during interview research, to imagine the apparently minor but still important ethical situations which arise. The respondent asks a question about the research process, and the researcher has to decide how to reply; the respondent asks to see a copy of the research data, or the respondent becomes slightly uncooperative – all of these situations may have an element of ethical decision-making. One of the areas which raises significant ethical issues is that of recording data.

It has become almost the norm nowadays that unstructured or semi-structured interviews are tape recorded. Videotaping can be used, and does have the advantage of being able to record physical gestures and facial expressions. Probably most research of this type, however, employs simple audio-taping. Note-taking cannot ensure the same degree of accuracy of recording the actual words spoken, let alone such often important matters as emphasis and pauses between utterances. The first thing to be said about tape recording is that the informed consent of the participant should be obtained. The researcher should explain to participants the reason for wishing to tape record the interview, the way in which the recordings will be used, the way in which the tapes will be stored, and the procedure for destruction of the tapes when all the data have been transcribed. Participants should also be informed of the way in which they will be identified on the tape. For example, the interviewer may accidentally refer to the interviewee by name during the recording, and participants may need reassuring that when data are transcribed, anonymity will be assured by using only fictional names. It may take some time to fully inform fully the prospective interviewee, but it is necessary to invest in this time, before asking for consent to the interview.

Researchers should also bear in mind that the use of the tape recorder may be slightly intimidating for many people, and distinctly worrying for a few. Some people may be concerned that they will say rather more than they would wish on a sensitive matter. In other cases, no matter how many reassurances are given about anonymity and confidentiality, some respondents may feel extremely nervous about having an interview tape recorded. There are several strategies which can be adopted to help ensure that most people feel happy and relaxed with the process.

A useful strategy is to place the tape or disc recorder within easy reach of the interviewee, and to explain to them before the interview starts that they may use the pause button at any time. In other words, the interviewee is given absolute control over the recording process. You can advise the interviewee that if at any time they need to consider their response to a particular question, then they can hold down the pause button in order to have time to reflect. They are also able to stop the recording of the session if they so wish.

Another possibility is to offer interviewees the opportunity to play back the tape or disc at the end of the interview. If at that stage they feel that some of what they have said does not reflect their real feelings, or is not expressed as accurately as they would like, then they can amplify this with further discussion. They can either add to the recording to try to explain their views more clearly, or selected words and sentences can be deleted from the recording. This should reassure most people who feel rather nervous about the process.

In fact, feeling a little uncertain about the tape recording of an interview is a perfectly understandable emotion. It is extremely difficult to answer questions spontaneously, and to express ourselves to our satisfaction, the first time that we try. It is rather like leaving a message on a telephone answering machine. I think most people (including myself) find this less than easy. After all, when we write or type our views about a topic, we can reread what we have written, and revise it. It is only fair that we offer participants in a research interview the same facilities. The important thing is to obtain data which reflect as accurately as possible the views of the participants.

There are a number of other issues which arise in the recording of data. For example, having a recorder present may affect the manner and content of what an interviewee says; they may be more reticent about what they say, than if the recorder were not present. However, this is less an ethical issue than one of validity. The principal matters, in an ethical sense, are that as researchers we take all reasonable measures to ensure the peace of mind, and fair treatment of the people we ask to help us with our research. (For the issue of recording data, see Punch 1998: 181–2.)

The right of respondents to end involvement in the research

It is arguably part of the principles of freedom and autonomy inherent in taking part in research that the participants should feel free to withdraw at any time. Even when participants give their informed consent, they cannot necessarily be expected to anticipate their feelings about participation. They cannot anticipate whether they will find the experience enjoyable or stressful. Some parts of the research process may prove to be disconcerting, for example in the case of being interviewed about one's personal feelings. It is important, that as part of the induction and informed consent process, participants are reassured that they may withdraw from the research at any time. They should not have to give any notice about withdrawal, and they should not have to provide any explanation. There should of course be no penalties for not continuing, and participants should not be brought under any pressure to continue.

One possible general cause for participants wishing to discontinue involvement, is that the circumstances of the research change. For a variety of reasons, the details of the research outlined in the informed consent process either alter or need to be altered by the researcher. The changes should be communicated to participants as soon as possible, and the informed consent be in effect renegotiated. No matter how carefully a piece of research is designed, it is seldom possible for researchers to plan all aspects of the project. Some features have to be adapted as the research actually progresses. If any of these changes are likely to have affected the original decision of participants to take part, the consent process must be revisited.

Sometimes participants can find that the research process suggests elements of their personalities or lives which they would prefer not to acknowledge. Such elements may not reflect reality, but nevertheless their imagined existence may be disconcerting. Such situations sometimes arise in research in psychology for example. Consider the case in Box 3.1.

The ethical issue here may revolve around the nature of the information given during the informed consent process, at the induction to the research. If the respondents were informed that they could leave the research at any time, that no questions would be asked, and no notice required, then it seems that the researchers have a moral duty to let the respondents leave as promised. On the other hand, if the promise of the freedom to leave had been made in a more general sense, there could be a case for at least checking that participants had an accurate understanding of the purpose of the research. However, this is conditional upon the participants not *assuming* that theirs was an unconditional right simply to walk out. If they gained the impression that there was possibly still a negotiation process to be completed before they

---

Box 3.1 Ethical dilemma: withdrawal from research

Two researchers are investigating the extent to which people can concentrate on relatively straightforward tasks over a specified period of time. The tasks involve maintaining a required orientation between several geometrical shapes on a computer screen. The shapes move apart at random, and the participants have to keep trying to bring the shapes back to their original orientation. The participants are of different ages, and one of the aims of the research is to investigate whether the ability to concentrate on such a task varies with age. This is explained in non-technical language to potential participants at the beginning of the research, and they appear perfectly happy. Some participants, from all age ranges, have difficulty with the tasks. Some of the older participants, however, claim that the research is 'just designed to show that older people lose their powers of concentration', and they leave the project. Others show signs of following them. The researchers are concerned, and wonder whether just to let people leave, or whether at least to try to have a discussion with them and to set their minds at rest.

---

could leave, then perhaps the researchers are entitled to explore briefly their understanding of the research project. However, it would seem completely unethical if any degree of persuasion were used. The ethical issue at stake is one of promise-keeping. It is concerned with promising people about the way in which you intend to treat them, and then ensuring that you do not deviate from your promise.

It can be seen from this situation that it often does help to write down precisely what will be said to potential participants during a research induction period. If the same language is used with everyone, as far as possible, then there is a relatively unambiguous record of what has been promised to people, and what has not been promised.

The disclosure by respondents of sensitive material

The process of data collection may result in participants discussing issues with the researcher, which are of a sensitive nature. Under such circumstances the researcher has the choice of treating such material simply as data, or of responding in some way. In the latter case, the researcher might feel an obligation to provide advice or information which might help the person concerned. Alternatively, the researcher might consider divulging the information to a third party. Such a course of action would be in clear breach of any promises of confidentiality, and could be contemplated only in exceptional circumstances. There is a detailed discussion of questions of anonymity and confidentiality in Chapter 5, but in the mean time, we can consider a situation in which the respondent starts to discuss a rather sensitive matter with the researcher, and where the researcher has a number of options (see Box 3.2).

Box 3.2   Ethical dilemma: responding to sensitive material

A researcher is interviewing employees within a large company operating in the financial services sector. The purpose of the research is to investigate the extent to which employees feel that their career aspirations are encouraged and supported by the company. The management of the company have provided all necessary facilities for the research. They are hoping to use the results to inform their human resources policy. The participants appear to feel that to a reasonable extent, the company tries to provide the necessary support for their career ambitions. However, one respondent, completely unexpectedly, alleges that he is bullied by his line manager. He claims that his work load is excessive compared with that of his colleagues, and that when he does not meet targets he is called into his manager's office and criticized using insulting terms. He asks the researcher not to say anything, as he fears retribution and cannot afford to risk losing his job. The researcher has received no indications of similar problems from other respondents, although the researcher does not thereby discount what the interviewee has said. The researcher wonders whether to respond, and if so, in what manner.

The researcher takes the view that if there is anything reasonable that can de done to improve the situation for the respondent, then the researcher should do it as a moral responsibility. However, the researcher is also aware of the plea by the respondent not to intervene with the line manager. The researcher considers the possible consequences of intervention, and decides that even if the wishes of the respondent were overlooked, the results of intervention with the line manager would be difficult to predict. The researcher therefore decides to examine other possibilities.

The researcher decides to discuss with the respondent the places and people he could go to for help, and forms the impression that the respondent has very little idea of where he could obtain advice. The researcher discusses the role of a professional association, and also mentions several types of advice agencies, but restricts these to the kind of information which would be available in principle to any member of the public who made general enquiries. The researcher considers offering personal advice on strategies for dealing with the manager in one-to-one situations, but decides against it on the grounds of not being qualified to give such advice, and that the consequences would again be unpredictable.

The disclosure of sensitive material can happen at any time in research, and the researcher in this example, in trying to decide on a course of action, has essentially attempted to consider the likely results of the possible actions. A philosophical analysis of such a type is termed consequentialist. Let us look briefly at this in Box 3.3.

Box 3.3   Theoretical perspective: consequentialism

This is the general view that if we wish to analyse whether a particular action is good or bad, then we should reflect upon the likely consequences of that act. According to this view, it is the consequences and not the act itself which determines the moral worth of the act. One form of consequentialism is that an action is considered good if its results are as equally good or better than any other potential actions. Another variant is that an action is considered good if it derives from a set of ethical rules whose application generally results in as much good or more good, than any other set of moral rules (see Nielson 1998: 142–51).

There are several variants of consequentialism and we shall return to this approach later in the book.

Ethical issues in the use of information and communication technology

The rapid expansion in the use of information and communication technology (ICT) in research has created a range of ethical concerns. These are possible to address, provided that care and sensitivity are displayed towards both respondents and fellow researchers.

Perhaps we can start with an apparently straightforward issue, the storage of data. With the help of ICT, research data can be stored and combined with other data in large quantities. Although this is a desirable and useful trend, we need to be aware of the ease with which others might be able to access the data. We may make copies of data, which become readily accessible to others who might use our computers. Discs storing confidential data are easy to lose, or to use for another purpose by another person. As researchers, it is important that we feel confident in assuring our respondents that any data stored electronically are secure, and cannot be accessed by a third party.

It is easy to transmit data, as say an email attachment, both nationally and internationally. Essentially, we have to continually remind ourselves that we should not be unduly influenced by the technology. If we would not use data in a certain way normally, then we should not do so using 'new' technology. The same basic principles of informed consent, anonymity and confidentiality still apply. We have to make certain that the technology which we use enables us to comply with these standards.

With the data analysis software, both quantitative and qualitative, which is available at the moment, it is easy to analyse large amounts of data, and to recombine that data in ways which would be time-consuming in pre-ICT days. Data may be collected for one study, and then combined and reanalysed for an entirely different piece of research. It is important to pause in such situations, and to ask ourselves whether the original providers of the data are aware of the uses to which it is being put. Was there informed consent for the present uses of the data? In addition (and this is less of an ethical issue than a methodological one) the researcher would need to be sure that the secondary use to which the data are put is valid in an epistemological sense.

Since communication by email has developed, it has evolved a style of communication all its own. Characterized by an informality, brevity and succinct style of expression, email can be a rapid and useful means of communication in research. Sometimes, however, that brevity results in a loss of precision in meaning. Similarly, the use of colloquial forms of language can subtly alter the intended meaning. Research is a field of activity which requires precise forms of communication, and care should be taken that no confusion arises from the use of more informal language. Besides, emails are forwarded to other recipients with great regularity, and this uncertainty about the ultimate destination of our communications suggests that it is wise to take care with style and precision of expression.

An important area of ICT which has an effect upon research activity is obtaining research articles from the Internet. Some academic journals offer selected issues on the Internet, while there is a growing number of journals which are available as exclusively online publications. These are likely to be fully refereed journals, hence readers know that published articles have been subjected to a careful quality assurance procedure. However, many other articles available on the Internet have not been refereed and hence may not be suitable as exemplars of their particular type of research. It is thus advisable when exploring the background to a particular research topic, or conducting a literature search, to try to ensure that you are using fully refereed articles. Of course, one can argue that there is always a moral responsibility upon those placing an academic article on the Internet, to be completely transparent about the origin of the article, and the extent to which it has been quality assured.

The ethics of ethnographic fieldwork

The ethnographic approach to research usually involves collecting data on social phenomena in their natural context, while trying to leave that context as undisturbed as possible. The natural context is often termed the 'field'. As such, ethnographic fieldwork is a very interesting area of social and educational research, but it does raise some important ethical issues.

In ethnographic fieldwork, the field itself can consist of a wide variety of situations. In the social anthropological sense, one might imagine field-work being conducted in a remote Indian village, or among a community of indigenous Australians in a geographically isolated setting. Fieldwork can also take place in urban settings. We might speak of fieldwork in an urban primary school or a community education centre. An ethnographer might be conducting a study of a suburban health centre. Almost any social setting can constitute a research field. The important aspect from an ethical point of view is the manner in which the researcher interacts with that field and with the social members who make up that setting.

One of the most important characteristics which it is helpful for the researcher to cultivate is a sensitivity to the research field. One can think of the researcher as an intruder into a social context, and therefore someone who has an obligation to disturb that context as little as possible. Almost inevitably, the researcher will have some impact on the setting. There is almost certain to be some interaction with the people who exist in that setting. Those people will have some effect upon the researcher, and the researcher some effect upon them. However, the impact upon the field should, as far as possible, be minimized.

There are a number of strategies which can be adopted to try to achieve this. Philosophically, one of the main approaches is to be accepting of the worldview of the members of the research field. The researcher does not challenge the accepted customs and value system, but tries to merge into the background, recording and noting the changing social events. The process of studying the field in its original state, while trying to change it as little as possible, is known as naturalism or naturalistic research. Related to this approach is that of participant observation. The researcher tries, through this methodology, to become an accepted member of the social context, and within that framework, to continue with the process of observation and data collection. The strategies of participant observation exist on a continuum, with at one extreme the researcher being predominantly a participant and conducting less observation, while at the other extreme, the researcher is less of a participant and far more of an observer.

The essential ethical issue of naturalistic observation is that of the extent to which the researcher accepts the existing social context, and particularly the norms and values inherent in that context. It is possible that the researcher does not find anything in these norms which conflict with their own values. For example, researchers may be conducting an ethnographic study of a school, and feel at ease with the ethos of the school and the manner in which staff relate to the students. However, in a different school, the researchers may witness what they regard as a rather oppressive regime. There may be situations where they feel that they would like to intervene between staff and students, yet they feel that as researchers they are obliged simply to observe and not engage in any formal interaction. It is in such situations that the philosophical distinction which is held between the participant role and the observer role becomes very important. Such situations can be thought of as creating a conflict of role, and it is desirable if researchers can try to analyse their position in relation to these issues before the research commences. If they can decide the extent to which they are prepared to become a participant, then some of the potential role conflict is dissipated.

A related issue in ethnographic fieldwork is that of ethnocentrism. This is a situation where members of one culture tend to apply their own cultural values when evaluating another culture. It is sometimes applied to a situation where European countries are making unwarranted assumptions about the cultures of some developing countries. In principle the term can be used of any country or culture which is reflecting on another culture. The ethical issue involved in ethnocentric judgements is that all cultures should be evaluated in their own terms, and within their own frame of reference. Some would argue that it is inappropriate to employ the norms of one culture to evaluate the norms of another, which raises the difficult question of relativism, and whether there are any absolute standards which may be used to evaluate all cultures.

It is important within ethnographic fieldwork to consider an issue which pervades this book, and that is informed consent. The preceding discussion largely places on one side issues about the consent of the respondents to provide data, but of course this is a key question in all social science research. In participant observation research it is important for researchers to analyse the extent to which they anticipate being participants and the extent to which they want to be pure observers or researchers. One of the fundamental problems is that once researchers inform participants about the research and their role, this has a weakening effect upon the naturalistic basis of the research. The setting can never be truly natural again. The researcher will never know whether the participants are acting in such a way as to impress or otherwise affect the researcher. On the other hand, if researchers attempt to infiltrate a research field without informing anyone, they must address the ethical issues inherent in covert research. These are discussed in the last section of this chapter.

When researchers are conducting field research they may find themselves in situations where there is a moral conflict between the participant and the researcher role. Consider a situation where two research students wish to research and write an ethnographic study of the social relations and practices in the kitchen of a busy restaurant. They obtain the permission of the restaurant owner to work on unskilled tasks in the kitchen in order to collect their data. The researchers insist that they should tell the other workers about their purpose in being there, and the manager agrees that this is only fair. The other workers agree that they do not object to the researchers being there, but jokingly add that they do not want anything which they say at times of stress being written down. The participant observation starts and goes well. However, the researchers soon observe practices which create an ethical dilemma. There is apparently an understanding with the manager that the staff can take home surplus food which is likely to be wasted, but it appears to the researchers that food is being taken home in quantities somewhat greater than could be justified. They discuss the way in which they intend to respond to this (see Box 3.4).

Box 3.4   Ethical dialogue: participant observation

A: We might be wrong of course. We don't know anything about catering. They might just be taking what is fair.

B: They could be, but it just seems over the top to me.

A: The main thing is that we should not get involved in it.

B: Agreed. But what if they ask us? It might be awkward for us if we refuse.

A: It probably would, but we would just have to insist.

B: What about telling the manager? Do you think we should mention it?

A: That would be really awkward for us! It would be different if we really knew they were doing something unfair or illegal, but we don't know. We might actually be wrong.

B: OK, agreed. We don't need to tell the manager, but what about writing up the data? The manager might ask to see the research report.

A: Well, we are not obliged to show it. However, I think we should just write it up as objectively as we can, but be very careful about the language we use. We can also ask our supervisor to check that part of the report very carefully.

The research students seem to have analysed the dilemma in a fairly balanced way, but this does illustrate how problems can arise during fieldwork. Small changes in the scenario can have a big effect upon the ethical dilemmas. For example, if the workers are seen to be taking rather more food, and it becomes clear that something dishonest is taking place, the position of the researchers changes. Similarly, if in this case they were pressurized to take food themselves, the situation changes once more. We can see that while ethnographic fieldwork is an interesting form of social science research, ethical problems can easily arise when they are least expected. (For a discussion of ethnographic fieldwork, see Fielding 1993: 169.)

The ethics of the research interview

The most common method used to collect interview data is the audiotape recording. This process raises a number of ethical issues, discussed in the first section of this chapter. Other ethical issues derive primarily from the process of holding a directed conversation with another person. At this stage it is worth remembering that the majority of research interviews have clearly defined purposes. The interviewer is setting out to collect data which relate to the research aims which have already been determined. It might be thought that with an open-ended, qualitative research design, research interviews do not have a precise purpose other than to collect data. It might be considered that their main function is just to enable the interviewee to talk about a topic. However, this is really a purpose in itself. In the early stages of a qualitative study, the researcher is often wanting to map out the issues which the interviewee defines as important, and the achievement of this is one of the principal aims of the research interview.

Researchers will thus have a list of key areas which they hope to discuss with the interviewee. On the one hand the list might be an interview schedule consisting of an actual list of questions which it is proposed to ask, while on the other hand, it might consist of a mental note of a few issues which it is hoped to raise. However the interviewer structures the interview, there may easily arise situations where the interviewer wonders whether to pursue a particular issue. It may be that the interviewee has appeared reluctant to discuss an issue, and the interviewer is doubtful whether to continue with the questions in this area. It may be that the interviewee feels uneasy discussing a particular topic, and the manner in which the researcher chooses to respond is clearly an ethical issue.

At the beginning of the interview the researcher may promise the interviewees that they can withdraw at any time, but it is important for this safeguard to work, that the interviewees have the confidence actually to articulate their feelings. To this end, it is a good idea if the researcher tries to be as sensitive as possible to issues arising which might be disconcerting for the interviewee. Then the researcher can ask if it is acceptable to continue with the present issue. This provides an opportunity for the interviewee to ask to be released from the interview.

One aspect of the research interview which is worth considering is that of the extent to which the interviewee gains something from the research process. Discussions of the interview process tend perhaps to concentrate upon the strategies used by the researcher to gain the required data. The focus is perhaps understandably upon the data-collection process, and ensuring that accepted ethical standards are adopted. However, it is worth pausing on the extent to which the respondents gain anything from the research process. Many people enjoy being interviewed. It is a process which places interviewees at the centre of considerations. It is their views that matter; their thoughts on an issue are being recorded, and a research report will be constructed around the data which they provide. It is also a process which enables and encourages interviewees to think out their own positions on complex issues. It is an opportunity to reflect on their values and opinions. There are no real distractions, and for a short period of time, it is their views which really matter.

It is arguably an ethical issue for the researcher to try to ensure that interviewees maximize the opportunities inherent in this situation, and gain something personally from this opportunity for reflection. It is not a question of the researcher encouraging the interviewee towards a particular viewpoint (and certainly not the viewpoint held by the researcher), but rather of trying to provide an opportunity for the interviewee to arrive at a personal position on a number of complex issues. In this way, the research interview is not merely a one-sided process, designed to help the researcher complete a research exercise, but rather a process of mutual help where the interviewee achieves a certain level of fulfilment through the exercise of reason and reflection. This is not entirely unrelated to the ethical position of helping people to realize their own potential, derived in part from the approach of Aristotle (see Box 3.5).

Box 3.5 Theoretical perspective: Aristotle and rationality

The notion of self-realization or self-actualization can be useful in considering how the interview process can help interviewees to gain something from the research process. Aristotle (384–322 BCE) argued that an important way in which human beings could achieve their potential was through the use of their powers of reason. An ethical dimension on the interview process would be to encourage respondents to view the interview as an opportunity to analyse and clarify their feelings about the issues raised (see Ross 1964: 232–4).

If interviewees can perceive the interview in this way, they can perhaps see it as an opportunity to gain an insight into themselves and their own value positions.

Ethical issues in the use of questionnaires

The use of self-completion questionnaires in survey research may not seem to raise many ethical issues, as there is little direct interaction between researcher and respondent. However, there are still potential areas of concern.

Let us consider the sampling process in a survey. The researcher often starts the research process by having an idea of the total research population. In the case of a survey of all primary schools in England, it would be possible to find out the total number of such schools, and also their names. In the case of a survey of all primary school teachers in England, it would again be possible (in theory) to find out the number and names of all such teachers. Instead of sending questionnaires to every separate member of the research population, the researcher may select a sample of that population to provide data. Again, the researcher would in principle know the identity of each member of the sample. It is conceivable that the researcher might simply send the questionnaire to 'The Head of Mathematics' at each school, without specifying a name. However, the name of the post-holder could be ascertained. The identification of the members of the sample is necessary for the straightforward reason of addressing correspondence.

Now suppose that only 50 per cent of the respondents return their questionnaires. The researcher will probably want to send a reminder to those who have not responded. But which 50 per cent? One solution would be to number or code the questionnaires, and for the researcher to retain a list of names and codes, enabling each questionnaire to be identified with a specific person. When a questionnaire is returned, the code and name could be deleted from the list, and the code removed from the questionnaire. That questionnaire could no longer be associated with a specific person, and the researcher would be left with a list of those people who had not returned questionnaires. They could then be circulated with a reminder.

However, assuming that respondents are promised anonymity, and told that they need not enter their name on the questionnaire, the above system should also be explained on the questionnaire or on an accompanying letter. Respondents should be reassured that the coding system will be deleted from every questionnaire returned. They should also be told that after a single reminder letter, the remaining list of codes and names will be destroyed. Hence, the researcher will have absolutely no record of who has or has not responded.

There are a number of variants, but it is important to explain the essentials of the system on the questionnaire or on an accompanying letter. This is, in a sense, part of an informed consent procedure. Any other information which is part of the informed consent procedure should be clearly set out in a letter. In addition, the instructions for completing the questionnaire should be clear and unambiguous. There is often a temptation with questionnaires to reduce the amount of text to be read by respondents, on the assumption that the effort of reading it might deter them from replying. Clearly, all researchers are interested in gaining as high a response rate as possible. From an ethical point of view, it is preferable to provide comprehensive information for respondents, and to risk losing a few replies, than it is to provide incomplete information for all respondents.

In terms of information to provide for respondents, it is probably desirable to include on the questionnaire a reminder that respondents do not need to answer any question which they consider inappropriate. They should be informed about mechanisms for storing the data, and for how long it is intended to keep it. It may also be relevant to explain which people will have access to the data, and broadly speaking how the data will be used.

It is a practical but also an ethical point that people do not generally wish to be involved in any expense in replying to a questionnaire. It is sufficient inconvenience to be asked to devote time to completing it. Hence, a reply-paid envelope should generally be included. As a general rule when designing survey research by questionnaire, it is a good idea to imagine your own feelings when an unsolicited questionnaire drops through your letter box. Try to put yourself in that position, and then think of as many ways as possible of putting the mind of the respondent at ease. (Ethical issues in survey research are discussed in Schutt 1996: 301.)

The use of inducements to provide data

Sometimes researchers or research organizations feel that it is appropriate to provide inducements to participants. One of the commonest is a small cash payment to recompense participants for the time expended in helping with the research. The argument here is that if people are asked to give up say an hour of their time to take part in a focus group or to be interviewed, then they should be paid in much the same way that someone who works for an hour is also paid.

Another form of inducement is to offer all participants the opportunity to have their names entered in a raffle, and to have the chance of winning a prize. Although not everyone can be recompensed by winning a prize, it may be an inducement to take part in the research, and thereby increase the number of participants.

On the face of it, these may seem reasonable strategies to adopt, but let us analyse them further. Perhaps we can start by revisiting the start of the relationship between researcher and participant. The researcher is seeking help with what one presumes to be a worthwhile activity (research), and asks the participant for assistance. The participant agrees, based on the information provided by the researcher. The researcher is usually grateful for the help, because they want to complete the research, while the participant could gain some satisfaction from providing the data, and has some interest in the subject of the study. In other words, this should be a symbiotic relationship in which both parties have something constructive to gain.

Supposing, however, that the researcher, when recruiting participants, offers to pay them for the time spent providing data. This could alter the

perception of the research process from both the researcher's and the participant's viewpoint. The researcher may be tempted to be not quite as careful
as before in explaining details of the research, on the grounds that 'Well, after
all, the participants are getting paid, they should just get on with it!' The
researcher may not think anything like this, but it is a possibility that
the researcher's attitude may move in this kind of direction.

The respondents, on the other hand, may decide to take part in the
research, when otherwise they would have refused. The money may sway
their decision. They may not have felt that they had been given enough
information about the research, but ignored this at the mention of
remuneration. Equally well, the payment of participants by the hour
may affect the amount of time they devote to providing data. It is a possibility
that consciously or subconsciously, they may either embellish or minimize
data. This may be a subtle reaction on the part of participants, scarcely
brought to consciousness, yet it may change the nature of the data which
are provided.

Of course, these consequences may never arise, or they may be so subtle
that they are never recognized. What we can probably say is that the introduction of inducements has the potential to alter both the relationship
between the researcher and respondent, and the nature of the data provided.
If it is at all possible it seems preferable to avoid the introduction of inducements, and to retain the relationship of one person responding to a request for
help from another. This may seem a rather idealistic position to adopt, but if it
is at all practical, it does avoid some of the pitfalls.

Is it ever ethical to collect data from respondents using deception or covert methods?

The use of covert methods in social science and educational research seems
antithetical to most of what has been said so far about the ethics of research.
It certainly is in contravention of that basic principle of informed consent.
However, before rejecting covert methods as completely unethical, we
should examine the type of situation in which it might be argued that it
was acceptable, and also explore the grounds for such an argument. (For a
discussion of covert methods, see Crow 2000: 74.)

Suppose that a research project was designed to investigate the extent of
age discrimination in employment practices. More specifically, the project
wished to investigate different types of retail outlets and to explore whether
they selectively recruited employees from a particular age band. Initially the
lead researchers adopted an open approach to the research, telephoning the
managers of a range of companies to ask for an appointment to discuss
recruitment practices. Let us suppose that in each case the company refused

to make an appointment, citing the reason that it was company policy not to discuss recruitment policy and strategies. The researchers continued to feel that based on anecdotal information, it was a reasonable hypothesis that some retail companies recruited employees of a certain age category. The researchers decided to employ covert methods, in order to investigate the recruitment strategies used.

They enlisted the help of a number of research students from the same university, who represented a wide range of different ages. They selected a sample of retail outlets different from those already approached. They then looked for advertisements for retail vacancies with these companies. Having identified a vacancy, students of different ages were asked to call at the company and ask for further details. Let us suppose that in many cases older applicants were told that a vacancy had been filled. Later, younger applicants were often given immediate interviews for these same jobs. The researchers felt that they had collected reasonable evidence to suggest that a degree of age discrimination existed in this employment sector.

In this imaginary case, let us consider briefly the kinds of justifications which the researchers might have offered for the use of covert research methods. First, they might have argued that the data could not have been collected in any other way. Similar companies had refused to divulge any data about their recruitment procedures, and it seemed likely that this was the only way to collect any empirical data. However, one could argue in reply that this is only a practical justification, and that if covert methods were employed whenever a data-collection procedure did not seem to be practical, then covert methods would be widely employed.

A second type of possible justification would be based upon the estimated results of the use of covert methods. At the moment, the researchers hypothesize that some companies selectively recruit people, using age as an important criterion. If this is the case, many well-qualified people may not have a fair chance of obtaining the kind of employment they would wish. They are being significantly disadvantaged. If the research could establish that this is the case, it may be possible to influence the employers to change their policy. The researchers may argue that the covert research has the potential to enhance the life chances and general happiness of many people. Although the method is in principle unethical, it would not appear that the employers are likely to be significantly harmed by the process. The researchers intend to preserve the anonymity of the companies and individuals. The justification of the covert research rests upon the argument that the approach appears likely on balance to increase the amount of happiness in society, while at the same time having no significant adverse effects. As this argument rests upon an analysis of the results of using the method, it is consequentialist in nature. It also illustrates a particular approach to ethical issues known as act utilitarianism. This approach is summarized in Box 3.6.

Box 3.6 Theoretical perspective: act utilitarianism

Act utilitarianism is a consequentialist approach to ethical decision-making, which suggests that in choosing how to act in the world, we should try to select that action which we estimate will produce the greatest amount of good. Of course, an action may not have exclusively good consequences. There may be some adverse consequences. The act utilitarian would select that act which appeared most likely to result in more beneficial than adverse consequences. The concept of 'good' is open to a number of different interpretations, and many act utilitarians have traditionally thought of this in terms of 'happiness'. It is often difficult to predict the extent of the consequences of an action, and which people will be affected by it. Act utilitarians often restrict their considerations of the balance of good and undesirable effects to those who are likely to be immediately affected by the action. Act utilitarianism is often associated historically with the work of, among others, Jeremy Bentham (1748–1832) (see Raphael 1981: 34–42).

If an act utilitarian were to support the use of covert methods in this instance, it might be on the grounds of the judgement that such methods are likely to result in the greatest happiness for future job applicants. However, this case study is far from simple. Although the research may arguably result in a fairer system of recruitment, there will inevitably remain some applicants who are successful and some who are unsuccessful. It is also difficult to estimate the consequences of actions, and to predict accurately the balance of good and undesirable results. There may well be unforeseen consequences resulting from any action.

In summary, it is difficult to avoid the view that covert methods are in principle unethical, and should normally be avoided. The justification of their use in specific and exceptional circumstances may be based upon a form of utilitarian argument. Nevertheless, the difficulty of predicting the consequences of using covert data-collection methods should cause us to exercise caution in the use of such approaches.

4 Research and the respondent

Ethical issues when data collection has been completed

The issue of allowing respondents to read, edit and confirm the accuracy of data

It is sometimes easy to imagine that the major ethical issues in research have been dealt with once the data-collection phase has been completed. However, there are many areas in which the ethical responsibilities of the researcher continue, and where problematic issues can arise, for example when research participants ask if they can check the accuracy of data after they have been collected. There may be nothing unreasonable about such a request, but as with many issues in research ethics, much depends upon the precise context.

The most straightforward situation is where a participant would like a copy of a completed questionnaire. People could clearly make themselves a copy of the questionnaire they have completed, and the researcher could provide a copy for them. However, no individual is entitled to questionnaires completed by other respondents. If people wish to gain an idea of the overall results from a survey, they should normally wait for the results to appear in the public domain. It would clearly be unethical for a researcher to pass on data provided by respondent A to respondent B, without the permission of respondent A.

The situation with regard to tape recordings of interviews is similar. It seems a reasonable request on the part of the respondent to receive a copy of the interview tape. However, there are different issues if the respondent asks to have a copy of the transcript of the tape. When an interview tape is being transcribed, the researcher performs interpretative work on the recording. The researcher listens not only to the actual words spoken, but also to matters of emphasis, pronunciation, pauses and tone. Researchers will usually encode these issues into the written transcript, as they may become significant in some types of analyses. It is possible that two researchers will listen to the same tape, and transcribe it in different ways. The basic words will be the same, but the manner in which the other features of the dialogue are encoded on the typed page may well be different. Two researchers not only may employ a different coding system, but also may interpret the same linguistic features in different ways.

Once the researcher has performed this type of interpretative work, the resulting analysis becomes, in a sense, the property of the researcher. At this stage of the analysis, there is arguably no obligation upon the researcher to pass on a copy of the analysis to the respondent. Some of this analysis may be included in, say, an academic article which passes into the public domain, and the respondent will then have an opportunity to read it. Within this broad area then, it seems reasonable to distinguish between the rights of the respondent in relation to raw data, and the rights in relation to data which have been subjected to analysis by the researcher.

A separate issue arises, however, where there is no clear record in writing or on tape. Such situations occur in the context of observational research, or generally where the researcher is keeping notes. In the case of observational research, the participant normally has no right of access to any of the data. The researcher will have performed interpretative work on the social context, in order to transform a variety of social interactions into research data which are ready for analysis. This process will inevitably have involved selectivity from the broad range of possible data, and hence there will have been a considerable impact by the researcher. If we wish to attribute moral ownership of such data, then it would appear to reside with the researcher. The only permission which the researcher is obliged to obtain under such circumstances is that of being allowed to be present as a researcher in that particular social context. Once that permission has been obtained then the researcher is free (subject to certain other ethical obligations detailed later) to collect such observational data as may be required.

This does not mean to say that the researcher is free to write absolutely anything in the field notes or observational records. The latter must represent a truthful record of events, as far as this is possible. This certainly begs the question of the meaning of 'truthful', and we must assume in the preceding argument that the researcher does not knowingly misrepresent what is happening in a social situation, or deliberately distort a series of social interactions. The researcher should also not be so selective in terms of data, that the picture which emerges is very far from reality as understood by most participants or observers.

There are also practical reasons for not encouraging or allowing participants to read and edit large amounts of primary data. First, it would be extremely time-consuming, and would prolong the data-analysis phase of the research. Second, participants may have different views about the accuracy and validity of the same section of the data. This could create situations which were very complex to resolve. Third, participants would not normally be trained in the procedures of social science research, and would not usually be equipped to appreciate the kind of analysis undertaken by the researcher. It would therefore not be appropriate to think of participants as being able to 'check' the data in any meaningful sense of the word.

Reporting research results to respondents

Some respondents will be sufficiently interested in the research to wish to see some of the results. While this is a reasonable request, it is important to clarify exactly what the respondents would like to see. They may wish to see, for example, the final report on the research. If it is intended that this will be an article in an academic journal, which is clearly in the public domain, there will be no difficulty. Those repondents who request it could be sent an offprint of the article. However, the findings may be recorded in a report which is initially destined for the sponsors of the research. If it was part of the original research contract that the report was the property of the sponsors, it would not be within the power of the researcher to release it to respondents.

Respondents may wish to see merely some of the interim results, to gain an idea of the kinds of conclusions that might be drawn from the research. While this may be a sufficiently innocent request, it is not always easy to define the status of interim results. If they are interim, they may not be thought out in a sufficiently clear manner; they may be based on only part of the total data; and they may differ considerably from the final research results. To release them, even to a small number of respondents, may be precipitate. Arguably there should be only one set of results from a research programme, and those results should be the final ones.

Research participants may have no clear ethical claim upon the results of a study, other than to read results when they have passed into the public domain. One could argue that participants have no particular moral claim upon the results, conferred by their role as participants. The rights of participants may be far more clearly associated with the manner in which they are informed about the research at the beginning, and the way in which their consent is obtained, rather than with being supplied with results from the research. (The issue of the availability of research results is discussed in Kane 1995: 213.)

Arrangements for the disposal of raw data

Social science and educational research generates considerable quantities of raw data. If we simply consider the number of tape recordings of interview data collected by university students for research projects in a single academic year, we will realize the potentially large quantity of raw data which exists. The disposal of raw data is an issue which should be discussed with research participants during the informed consent procedure. They should be informed about the way in which the data will be used; whether data will be retained in some form of database; finally, if it is intended to dispose of the data, then participants should be informed of the procedure and of the time-scale. Some researchers do not discuss this with participants, yet it remains an important issue.

The first stage in the process is that the researcher should ideally have anticipated the issue and have developed a clear policy. This should then be conveyed to the participant during the informed consent procedure, and following the analysis of the data, the researcher should clearly adhere to the policy. If the policy is that data will be destroyed following analysis, it is important to consider the process and time-scale for this. If the decision is simply to destroy paper-based or electronic data, this can be achieved at one time. However, if it is decided to record over audiotapes, this process may take place over a period of time. The researcher might decide to retain the raw data for some period after the completion of the thesis or the research report, in case there are questions raised about some of the analysis.

It may be decided to retain the raw data as a complete data set. There may be a variety of legitimate reasons for this. The researcher may prefer to have the data set still in existence, in order that other researchers will be able to replicate the analysis if necessary. The researcher may feel that someone else may wish to analyse the same data in a different way for a separate research project. Whatever the reason for retaining the data, there are a number of basic precautions which should be taken by the researcher.

Where the data were collected solely for the researcher's own use, they may have included names or other means of identification within the data. If there is any possibility that someone else may have access to the data, all means of identification should be removed. Sometimes databases may be stored electronically within an institution, in such a manner that other people may gain access to them. All reasonable precautions should be taken to ensure that individuals cannot gain access to the database by accident, and that all access is as a result of a deliberate application through formally established channels. It is possible that the original researcher may move posts or departments within an institution, and the databases may be capable of being accessed via the researcher's former computer. All necessary precautions should be taken to try to maintain the integrity of the database, and to ensure that if anyone gains access to it, whether authorized or not, that it is not possible to identify individuals within the data set. Difficulties can sometimes arise with preserved data sets, where some of the data have been used, and the remainder have not been utilized (see Box 4.1).

Box 4.1 Ethical dilemma: preserving a data set

Two researchers have been collecting life-history data on the careers of a large sample of school teachers. The original purpose of the research was to be a book discussing teacher careers. This was explained to respondents during the process of informed consent. The respondents were guaranteed anonymity in the final accounts, along with a promise that the schools in which they taught would also be described using fictional names. The book was written and eventually published. However, the researchers used only a part of the total data collected, and decided that the remaining data could be used as the basis for several academic journal articles and conference papers. They had promised respondents that the data would be used for the book and then destroyed. They wonder whether it would be ethical to retain the data, and use it for some articles and conferences, as long as they continue to adhere to the established principles of anonymity. They would normally not hesitate to contact all of the teachers, but since the data were collected they are fairly sure a number have retired, and others have moved jobs. As a large number of respondents was involved, it would be a lengthy process to try to contact them all.

The uncertainty of the researchers in this situation arises because they are contemplating using a pragmatic justification to resolve their ethical dilemma. They are profoundly aware of having made a clear promise and of the imperative to adhere to that promise. They also know that if they wanted to write the journal articles, they should have asked for the permission of the respondents in the normal way. The researchers realize that now it would be extremely difficult to contact every teacher within a reasonable period of time, and hence are considering a pragmatic solution. This solution clearly involves breaking a promise, yet the justification is based upon the supposed permission which would be given by the respondents.

Common sense suggests that if the respondents did not mind the book being written, along with the associated guarantees of anonymity, they would not mind the articles or conference papers being written. The researchers cannot imagine any way in which the respondents could be harmed by the articles, and feel that to some extent, it is being ethically fastidious to feel they have to contact all the respondents for their permission.

Nevertheless, a promise has been made, and it seems unsatisfactory to ignore it. Eventually, the researchers reach a compromise in which they send a circular letter to all the schools in which respondents taught, and ask for the letters to be forwarded to any teachers who have left. In the letter, they ask for permission to use the data for the articles, and offer the same guarantees of anonymity. They provide reply slips and pre-paid envelopes. In order to ensure that the consultation process has a finite end, they say that if they have not received a reply by a specified date, they will proceed with the writing of the articles. On the other hand, if anyone replies saying that they do not wish their data to be used, that data will be extracted from the database and destroyed immediately.

Potential psychological effects on respondents

For most people it is not a very common experience to take part in a research project. It is an experience that the participant will probably remember, and one which may have psychological effects, some beneficial and some perhaps less positive. Let us consider the more positive effects first.

The role of the research participant is one in which essentially the researcher values what the participant has to say on an issue, and wishes to explore the values and opinions of the participant. If you are a research participant, a group of well-educated people spend considerable time listening to your opinions on issues, or reading your responses to a series of questions on a questionnaire. It is usually encouraging to think that people are interested in what we think, and in our values and opinions, and perhaps this is even more so in the context of a research programme. Thus the role of research participant is one which can help to create a feeling of well-being and self-confidence, and of being valued by others.

There is another potential advantage to being a research participant: it can help people to understand more about the dilemmas and conflicts which confront us in life. The role of the research respondent involves considering and reflecting upon what are usually fairly complex issues, and then trying to convey one's thoughts to the researcher. This may be in either the written or the spoken form. Almost inevitably, the respondent does learn from this process. The process of reflection may help them to clarify their own thoughts, and to be able to express them with greater lucidity.

Nevertheless, there are a number of potentially less desirable consequences to the process of research participation. Some educational and social science research concerns issues which are complex and somewhat disturbing. Such issues might include bullying, violence, theft, drug-taking and abuse of various kinds. Some research on these topics may inevitably involve asking questions of people who have been involved, in one capacity or another, in such activities. Such questions might very well invite people to recollect events which they have moved to the back of their consciousness and tried to forget. Consider the ethical dialogue in Box 4.2 between two researchers who are planning some research on the subject of school bullying.

Box 4.2   Ethical dialogue: researching potentially disturbing issues

---

A: Ideally it would be helpful if we could collect data from people who had been bullied at school, and also those who had done the bullying.

B: That's definitely what we would like, but how old should the respondents be in our sample?

A: Well, I'm a bit concerned if they are only a few years older than when the event occurred. They could still be very much emotionally involved with the event. They might lack that distance and objectivity needed to reflect on it.

B: If we interviewed teenagers who were fairly close to the event, we might get a real sense of immediacy with the data, but many of them might find the experience very difficult to cope with. The events could be still so traumatic that they just cannot discuss them.

A: That's true. It's rather difficult, because in some cases, to actually discuss the issue, might help the person. On the other hand, we are not trying to be counsellors here.

B: Well, that's right. I tend to prefer mature respondents. I'm fairly sure, with bullying, that they will be able to remember many of the events, and talk about them meaningfully.

A: Hopefully, they will be able to look back on themselves as a child, and reflect upon their situation in a way that a younger person could not manage. I think there's much less risk of any psychological ill-effects, and that must be an important consideration.

B: Absolutely. This topic will not be easy for anyone to talk about, and we have to do everything possible to enable it to be treated in a calm, objective manner.

A: One way of looking at it is that we would like them to remember the feelings they had at the time, but we don't want them to actually relive those feelings in an experiential way.

From time to time, social and educational research involves the exploration of disturbing issues, if only to try to understand and minimize the social consequences of rather disturbing phenomena. Such research, as in the case of research on bullying, may involve asking respondents to recall unpleasant events. The researchers in this dialogue propose to reduce the risk of unpleasant psychological consequences by restricting the sample to adults, who it is hoped will be able to take a balanced, objective view of events some time ago in their childhood. From an ethical viewpoint, this seems a useful strategy, although the data may well lose some of the intensity of feeling of data which might be collected from younger respondents. It is possible that younger respondents would actually not feel able to provide very much data, simply because they remained disturbed by their experiences.

A general effect of research, particularly research involving in-depth interviewing or other techniques intended to record the deeper feelings of people, is that there is a sense of intrusion into one's private world. The participant may feel that to varying degrees their privacy has been invaded. This could result from the feeling that they have been asked questions about very personal feelings, which they would not normally divulge except to close friends. Yet, as respondents, they are revealing these deep feelings to a complete stranger, who will include them in a written account. The respondents are probably aware that the written account may be read by a much larger group of people.

The feelings of the respondents that they have been intruded upon can be reduced by suitable measures at the commencement of the research. Let us imagine a case where former patients who have all suffered from a particular illness are interviewed in order to ascertain their experiences of treatment in hospital. This could result in their discussing a very personal and perhaps traumatic period in their lives. If the purpose of the research is to try to improve the manner in which other patients are treated in hospital, and this is fully explained to the respondents, then they may be reassured by the social utility of the research. In general terms, if research participants feel that the data which they contribute will be devoted to a socially useful purpose, this may help assuage any feelings of intrusion.

Research respondents can feel disturbed when they are selected in circumstances where they have little choice but to take part in the research. For example, if parents of children in a school were asked by teachers conducting some research to provide data or to take part in research interviews, they may feel disposed to agree, even though they would prefer not to be involved. They might agree because they would wish to support or assist the teachers of their children. The ethical problem is that although the parents are autonomous adults, their decision-making is not entirely free. They are constrained by a wish to support their children, and irrespective of their feelings about participation, they may be swayed by the desire to support the teachers and the school. The long-term consequence of this, however, may be that the parents feel that the researchers have taken advantage of them.

The central issue is one of moral autonomy, and the need for people to be able to take ethical decisions, untrammelled by extraneous considerations. They should be able to focus solely upon the ethical decision and any other relevant factors. It is not always possible to separate neatly the research activity from other factors. Whenever a teacher is acting as a researcher, and asks pupils to contribute data to a research study, there is an ambiguity of roles. Some pupils may agree to take part, when actually they would prefer not to be involved. The issue for the researcher is to try to ensure that all potential respondents feel that they have the freedom to refuse to take part, if that is their wish.

Social researchers can never be absolutely certain about potential consequences for participants, once the research is completed. In practical terms it may be unrealistic for researchers to try to monitor such consequences. What is important is that every effort is made to conduct the research in an ethical manner, in the hope that this will minimize any adverse consequences. A sensitive approach during the data collection may go a long way to reducing any ill effects later. (Potential effects on respondents are discussed in Stangor 1998: 39.)

The distinction between interview research and counselling

Researchers work within the parameters of the role of social scientist; the combination of this role with any other may lead to difficulties and confusion. This role conflict may arise if the respondent asks for help from the researcher, in an area outside the precise remit of the research. The respondent may view the researcher as a potential friend who is well educated and assumed to be in a position to offer personal help and advice. The respondent may use the opportunity of providing data in an interview to alter subtly the nature of the discussion, from one of providing information to one of seeking guidance. There may be nothing ill intentioned about this, because the respondent may not have reflected upon the complexities of the roles involved. However, researchers should anticipate such difficulties, and be prepared with an appropriate response.

Potential problems can arise without any warning. A respondent may suddenly confess that they are involved with substance abuse, and ask for help. Another respondent may say that they are the victim of physical abuse, and ask for advice. In a study of the accommodation needs of higher education students, one respondent may ask for advice on the best way of managing their student loan. The possibilities are numerous.

The ethical issues arising here are that first the research interview is not the appropriate location to discuss complex personal matters, and that second, the researcher is unlikely to be qualified to provide the specialist advice needed. Moreover, for many such issues the respondent both needs and deserves the advice of a qualified practitioner who society deems appropriate to give specialist advice. Normally, an appropriate response would be to advise the respondent to make contact with a suitable professional or agency. The researcher may not know precisely who might be a suitable professional, but could at least direct the respondent to a source of information.

If the researcher does not follow a procedure of this broad type, there is a danger that precipitate advice may be given, when the issue merits more careful reflection. It is possible that participation in research may be therapeutic for the respondent, but this is not the purpose of the researcher. Any such effects should be incidental to the main process of providing and collecting data. The researcher should not make a specific attempt to provide therapy or counselling.

On occasion, the researcher may be tempted to share an anecdote or personal experience with the respondent. This could happen in an unstructured interview situation. The researcher might relate an anecdote partly to establish a sense of empathy with the interviewee, and partly to encourage the interviewee to talk more. The technique may be well motivated, but it could lead to potential role confusion in the mind of the respondent. Consider the situation in Box 4.3, which (like the ethical dialogue in Box 4.2) involves a research project on the subject of school bullying.

Box 4.3   Ethical dilemma: sharing a common experience with the respondent

---

A researcher is using semi-structured interviews to collect data on respondents' experiences of being bullied while at school. During one interview the respondent is not very forthcoming, and appears to find it difficult to talk about his experiences. The researcher, who was also bullied at school to some extent, decides to share those experiences with the respondent. After the researcher has outlined one or two of his own experiences, the respondent starts to talk much more. He starts visibly to relax, and in fact provides very detailed accounts of the circumstances surrounding his being bullied. The researcher is pleased that his own account has apparently helped the respondent to discuss his own experiences, but the researcher is slightly concerned that he has influenced the respondent to say rather more than he would have otherwise preferred.

The ethics of this dilemma do not seem particularly clear; it may be that the researcher is being unnecessarily sensitive to the issue. However, the principle of social science and educational research is that the participant is willing to take part in the research, and decides as an autonomous individual exactly the type of data to provide. There should be no form of persuasion of any type, to provide more or less data, or data of one type or another. Questions are asked of the participant, and the participant provides the reply which they consider appropriate. Arguably, it is the role of the researcher to ask questions and not to provide data. If the contribution of data by the researcher in effect encourages the participant to provide different types of data, this could be perceived by some as being unethical. One could perhaps reduce this question to the issue of whether the participant is genuinely free to act as an autonomous agent. (The extent to which researchers should help or counsel participants is discussed in Knight 2002: 171–2.)

Possible consequences when the respondent remains in the research context

Social science research often involves the participant in divulging personal thoughts on complex and sensitive matters. There is not necessarily a problem with this, as long as the researcher complies with the appropriate protocols, and the participant is aware in advance that sensitive matters may be discussed. When the data-collection process has been completed, it may be that the researcher and the participant do not see each other again. If they remain in the same social milieu, however, the situation is different. The researcher now knows something of the values and attitudes of the participant towards a possibly sensitive issue. Under normal circumstances, the researcher would not have access to this information. The participant probably does not know the attitude of the researcher towards the same issue, since the researcher will not have divulged this during the research process. All is still well, provided that the researcher does not accidentally divulge any of the confidential information. One problem may be that with the passage of time, it is often difficult to remember where one first learned something. It is then relatively easy to divulge information without the deliberate intention to break a confidence.

This type of situation is particularly complex when research has been conducted in a work situation, with one employee as researcher and other employees as participants. At work people often have a number of social roles. This is particularly true in educational contexts. Consider the network of competing obligations which result from the professional relationships described in Box 4.4.

The holding of multiple roles is common in education, and may create difficulties in terms of research. When Sandra is being interviewed by Richard it will be difficult for her to act purely as a research participant without being conscious of her professional role. Any comments which she makes on staff development could have relevance for Richard's part-time course. If Sandra comments on the departmental policy about providing financial support for colleagues, there will be direct implications for Richard. When the data collection has been completed, the fact that Richard and Sandra often work together may make it difficult for the roles of researcher, respondent and colleague to be separated. Let us suppose that Richard does not receive financial support for his master's degree during the next academic year. In such a case it might be easy for him to remind Sandra of something which she said on the staff development issue during the interview. Equally, when Sandra is writing a reference for Richard, it might be easy to comment on an issue which arose in the interview.

Some people may feel that it is unrealistic to expect a complete separation

---

Box 4.4   Ethical dilemma: competing professional relationships

---

Consider the social roles occupied by two employees in a college. Sandra is a head of department, and Richard is a lecturer in that department. Sandra and Richard teach together on the course for which Richard is the course leader. Richard is enrolled as a part-time student for an MEd degree at a local university. He is at the thesis stage and the subject of his research is staff development policy in five different colleges, including the one in which he teaches. As part of the research, he interviews Sandra. In her role as head of department, Sandra is the budget-holder for the departmental staff development fund, and has considerable influence in deciding which staff should receive some financial support each year for their part-time study. Richard has developed some considerable expertise in information technology, and Sandra often asks for his help and advice when she has problems with her computer. Richard has recently applied for a promotion in a different department of the college, and has asked Sandra if she will act as a referee.

---

between the different roles. Nevertheless, it is something to which researchers should aspire. Perhaps the ideal situation is where there is in effect a mental barrier between the research activity and the other relationships and roles in which the researcher and participants are involved. The onus in trying to create this barrier should arguably rest with the researcher, who should be well versed in these issues. At the beginning of the interview or other data-collection event, the researcher could propose that the content of the interview not be discussed afterwards, either between interviewer and interviewee, or with any other person. This could be treated as part of an issue about confidentiality.

This chapter has been concerned with potential consequences once the data collection has been completed. Although it would be difficult for researchers to monitor such consequences, one possibility is to consider the use of a survey some time after the research has ended. Participants could be asked by interview or questionnaire whether, in retrospect, they had any comments to make on the research process. While this may not reveal all potential difficulties, it may help researchers to appreciate some of the longer-term consequences of research. It demonstrates a commitment, not simply to completing the research process, but to the welfare of those who have been kind enough to provide the research data.

PART 2
Ethical themes

5 The privacy of respondents, and restrictions on the use of data

Anonymity

A cornerstone of research ethics is that respondents should be offered the opportunity to have their identity hidden in a research report. There are a number of advantages for both researcher and respondents in the use of anonymity, but respondents do not always wish to take advantage of a hidden identity. Before we examine the more usual situation where respondents choose anonymity, let us explore briefly the kinds of situations where respondents prefer their identity to be known.

An individual or an organization may prefer that their identity is given in a report because they see some advantage in the associated publicity. After all, people are interviewed in the media all the time, and they are often identified. We can perhaps think of situations in education and social science research where a respondent may wish to be identified. A headteacher who is an advocate of a particular model of pastoral care in their school might welcome the opportunity to be interviewed as part of a research project, because it might provide a forum for discussion of this educational theory. A large organization which has agreed to take part in a study of its personnel policy might be happy to be named, if it feels that its policy is worthy of wider dissemination. Such a decision may seem appropriate at the time it is made, but later it may cause both researcher and respondent some concern.

The respondent, either individual or organization, may begin to realize that the data being collected are not entirely complimentary. They may begin to wish that they had some control over the data collection and over the way the report is written. However, this would not normally be part of the original research agreement. From the researcher's point of view, there may be related pressures. The researcher may be aware that some data do not portray a respondent in a flattering way, and may even come under pressure to exclude some data. The researcher may be concerned that when the research report is published, some respondents may claim that the research methodology was flawed, and that the respondents have not been portrayed fairly.

These potential problems illustrate the advantages of anonymity. One possible solution in the case of respondents who express a wish to be identified in a research report is to draw up a written agreement which sets down some of the main responsibilities of the research relationship. When the research programme is first being discussed with respondents, it could be pointed out to them that if their identity is maintained, this does not alter the freedom of the researcher to conduct the research as planned, and to write the report in a manner which is objective in the view of the researcher. The agreement would need to set down very precisely the methodology to be used by the researcher, and the main assumptions behind the data analysis. Such an agreement might eliminate some sources of misunderstanding, but research produces complex situations, and it is not always easy to anticipate areas of difficulty. We can already begin to appreciate some advantages of the use of anonymity in research. Let us examine these advantages systematically.

One of the principal advantages of anonymity in the dissemination of research is that it encourages objectivity throughout the research process. In social science and educational research both the researcher and the respondents are almost inevitably affected by the context in which the research takes place. If respondents are asked for their opinions about a medieval painting, say, there may be few implications in terms of offending people. The artist will not be alive, and it is unlikely that any descendants would be concerned about views on a painting from several centuries before. The respondents would feel relatively free to express their feelings in an objective manner, subject to any legal constraints on inappropriate language in a public place.

It could be a different situation, however, if respondents were asked for their views on the human resource policy of the large company where they were employed. They may have clear views on the policy, but if they thought that they would be identified, they may be cautious at revealing their true feelings. Promises of anonymity could make them feel sufficiently confident to be objective in their views. The anonymity frees them to express their true feelings.

From the perspective of the researcher, anonymity makes it easier to explore issues which might be slightly unpopular or which are regarded as sensitive. If the respondents are protected through anonymity, the researcher will feel more justified in being able to explore sensitive issues. The assumption will be that the respondents may be more willing to provide data in such circumstances.

Various methods can be used to anonymize a research report. One can remove all names and simply refer to respondents by numbers or letters, but this does tend to make the research account seem impersonal. It is difficult for the reader to relate to the individual respondents and what has been said, or to make a connection between a particular viewpoint and a specific respondent. It is easier to achieve this if fictional names are used. There are a number of issues with the use of fictional names. It may be important in terms of the credibility of the account to employ names of the same gender as the real respondent. With respondents from different ethnic groups, appropriate names should be are chosen. In the case of respondents from the Indian subcontinent, for example, there are some names which are characteristic of different regions of India, and some names which are characteristic of different religions, such as Hinduism, Sikhism and Islam. It is necessary for the authenticity of the research report to ensure that appropriate fictional names are selected, which may entail some research into the ethnic background and culture of the respondents in the sample.

In some research accounts there may be a tension between the attempt to achieve authenticity of names, and the desire to maintain anonymity. For example, when describing research in an organization in which there are very few men, the use of male fictional names may help to reveal their identities, and similarly where there are very few employees of a particular ethnicity. The very small number of participants of a particular group may make it difficult to maintain anonymity. Where this is the case, it may be preferable to employ numbers or letters to signify all respondents. It is a difficult decision, and the particular features of each situation will need to be considered.

Whether fictional names, letters or numbers are used to anonymize participants, it is often necessary during the writing of a research report or thesis for the researcher to maintain two parallel lists, one of the real names and one of the coded names. The researcher usually needs to do this in order to remember which participant is being discussed. Once the report or thesis has been completed, the coded list has to be destroyed. The real identities of the participants are then located only in the memory of the researcher, and these memories will fade in the fullness of time.

When research is undertaken in an organization such as a school, college or industrial company, it is often necessary to describe some features of that organization. If this is done with care, such descriptions, combined with a fictional name, should not reveal the identity of the institution. The description of an institution is often needed to clarify the social context in which the data have been gathered. In the case of a high school, it may be appropriate to describe the broad social class of the catchment area, to define the geographical area in which the school is located and to specify some features of school performance, for example in recent quality audits. In a comparable way, it may be necessary to describe some aspects of individual participants in relation to the organization in which they work. If one of the participants in a research study was the headteacher, it is almost certain to be relevant to mention this. Similarly, another participant may be the head of mathematics, or the sports coach. The full details of the post held by a participant should normally be given if they are specifically relevant to the research report. Otherwise, it may be possible simply to describe someone as a head of department or as a subject teacher.

If the anonymizing is carried out carefully, there should be no reason why any respondent could be recognized. The only way in which this might occur is by means of the identity of the researcher. If it is a full-time researcher who has no other connection or affiliation with the institution where data have been collected, the identities of respondents will normally be secure. However, if the researcher is also a teacher or other employee at an institution, and if this is stated in the thesis or research report, there is a clear connection whereby someone might be able to identify at least some of the respondents. Normally, researchers do wish to be identified, in their capacity as the author of a thesis or academic journal article. Once the thesis is placed in a library, or the article published, it may be possible for key figures in the research report to be identified.

Suppose a respondent is identified as the head of music in a high school. If someone read the thesis and was acquainted with the researcher, they might be able to identify the school, even though it had been given a fictional name. Knowing the approximate date at which the research had been conducted, it could be possible to identify the person who had been the head of music at the time. Nevertheless, it would take a certain amount of effort and determination to uncover the identities of people. It would be more difficult to identify respondents who did not hold a particular post. If some of the respondents had been pupils at the school, it would be difficult to identify them with any degree of certainty. This would still be so even if they were identified as being members of a specific year group.

In summary, the use of fictional names should go some considerable way to helping to ensure anonymity. There are no absolute guarantees of anonymity, particularly in the case of people who hold named posts, but the important issue is that researchers recognize the importance of privacy for respondents and then do their best to ensure that privacy. They may not always be absolutely successful, but the strategies described here go a long way towards that aim.

Another advantage of anonymity is that it protects individuals who may be mentioned by research respondents. It would be unfair if individuals unconnected to the original research project are identified simply because they are included in the discussion by respondents. If the respondent actually names people, they could be given fictional names in the same way as respondents. If the researcher considered that there was any risk of their being identified, it may be necessary to edit the data in such a way as to ensure anonymity. In order to preserve the validity and objectivity of the data, it may be necessary to explain the action taken at some point in the report.

One final issue about the use of anonymity is that it should not be used as a shield for making unfair or unjustifiable comments about people or organizations. When respondents are informed that as far as possible their identities will be hidden, they may feel liberated and uninhibited with their comments on the research issues. They should perhaps be cautioned that they should try at all times to be as objective and balanced as they can in what they say. If the researcher feels that some remarks are so unacceptable that they could not be included in the research report, a decision should perhaps be taken to exclude them, and an explanation provided in the report or thesis.

The editing of data raises complicated ethical questions. In the ethical dialogue in Box 5.1, the two researchers involved have collected some interview data from pupils in a high school, and debate whether some of it is appropriate to include in the official research report.

Researcher A is arguing that there should exist the potential for all data to be included in the final analysis of research. This argument depends to some extent upon the sampling method used for a research study. If a random sampling strategy has been employed, then every member of the research population should in principle have the same chance of being included in the sample. Hence, one might argue that there are no grounds for omitting the data from a single respondent. However, in the case of a purposive sample, where more subjective criteria may have been used in selection, one might feel that the subjectivity employed provides at least some justification for an element of subjectivity in the selection of data. The separate but related issue is that of the degree of freedom one should give respondents to use uninhibited language. The ethical issue would appear to be that people do not generally have the right to use insulting or unpleasant language to describe another person, when they could convey the same attitudes or beliefs in more balanced, objective language. Arguably, researchers should seek to find a way to report the ideas intended, in as balanced a manner as possible. This seems reasonable even in the case where researchers have done their best to ensure anonymity.

Confidentiality

It may help in the discussion of confidentiality if we begin with a brief analysis of the conceptual territory covered by the term, and of the way in which it relates to anonymity. Perhaps the starting point for a discussion of confidentiality is the idea of privacy. At first glance it does seem reasonable that people should be entitled to privacy, but perhaps the idea requires further examination. In rather general, theoretical terms we may assume that the concept of privacy is concerned with our private details and information not being

---

Box 5.1 Ethical dialogue: the editing of data

A: This group of four pupils have had a real go at the school! They obviously hate everything about it. Hardly a teacher escapes, and they've really been quite harsh about the head.

B: Do you think he's really that bad?

A: Well, as far as I can see there are no other pupils who have been anywhere near as critical and quite a lot are obviously happy at the school.

B: Maybe we should consider whether they are so atypical that we leave them out of the data.

A: I don't really like excluding them from the data. After all, the selection of respondents was more or less random. We had no idea who we were getting in the sample.

B: Well, there is first the issue about whether this group is so exceptional that we should consider how much credence to give their data. But second, they have used very strong language about the head, and I'm not sure whether we ought to include such language in our report.

A: OK, I agree it's a bit over the top. We could omit the sections with strong language, and just paraphrase what they said. Alternatively, we could just delete the offending words, and mark them with dashes. I still think we should include the data, in the sense that what they have to say may not be entirely typical, but it does indicate a particular point of view in the school.

B: I suppose so. We do know these pupils have been in some trouble in the past, and my guess is that they are using this research as an opportunity to get back at the school. I suppose what you're saying is that even if that is true, it is still significant that there are such strong pupil attitudes in the school.

A: I think so, yes. I just think that all data should potentially be used. We obviously have to be selective, but that selectivity is perhaps more about reducing the scale of the data, rather than choosing deliberately to omit particular views.

B: OK, I'm happy if we make sure we omit the really offensive language; but I accept we need to represent the views in some way.

---

circulated to others, and that in this sense privacy is a right, akin to other human rights. What, however, do we mean by a right (see Box 5.2)?

It is an arguable contention that privacy is not a fundamental moral right, but a feature of our lives which is allowed us by others. Similarly, it may be that confidentiality is something which we are promised, and at the same time, as part of that promise, we may be informed of the key methods by which that confidentiality will be ensured. Anonymity is normally one of those key methods.

Discussion of confidentiality is part of the informed consent process. However, it is important that researchers are explicit about all the elements of

---

Box 5.2   Theoretical perspective: rights and obligations

It can be argued that as human beings we possess certain moral rights, such as freedom for instance, which accrue to us by virtue of our basic humanity. Such rights are not given to us by others, but belong to us. They may be taken away from us, either temporarily or permanently, but that does not in a sense remove those rights. One might argue that even though we may be falsely imprisoned, and in a practical sense be deprived of our freedom, that in no way invalidates the freedom we possess as a thinking, reasoning human being. We are still, even in these adverse circumstances, free to think what we will.

It may not be quite as clear, however, that we possess the right to privacy, in the same way that we possess a right to freedom. As fundamentally social animals, perhaps privacy is subtly different from freedom, and is rather more a feature of existence which may be given to us by others. Someone may promise us that they will leave us in solitude, and not distribute any information about us; arguably in such a case, they have an obligation to help maintain our privacy. It is, however, an arguable question whether we actually possessed that right to privacy in the first place (see Mackie 1977: 172).

---

the confidentiality promise. It is simply not sufficient that the researcher promises to the respondent to keep the data confidential. First, there should be an explicit statement about the people who will have access to the data provided by a particular respondent; it should be clear about the people who will be able to read and scrutinize the data provided. Second, the respondent should be informed about the plans for retaining the data, and for providing access to other researchers during that period. The respondent should have a clear and unambiguous understanding of those people who will see the information they will be asked to provide and they should be informed about the procedures to be used to try to ensure that the identities of respondents remain undisclosed. In the case of questionnaire data particularly, the researcher may have the intention of combining data, such that individual respondents are subsumed under the total aggregated data. This is an alternative technique to the use of fictional names, to try to ensure anonymity. It is, however, suitable for only certain types of data.

This type of detail about the proposed plans for confidentiality should normally be made clear to potential respondents before they are asked to give their informed consent to participation in the research. Only with this level of detail can they be regarded as fully informed. The statements about confidentiality should be regarded as a promise, and treated with all the seriousness which that implies from a moral point of view. One cannot of course predict the nature of the data that will be provided in any research study, and the requirements of the law should carry precedence over promises made in such situations. Such precedence will usually involve matters of apparent criminal wrongdoing. (For discussions on anonymity and confidentiality, see Kvale 1996: 109–23; Aldridge and Levine 2001: 111.)

Trying to maintain the social ecology of a research setting

The social ecology of a setting refers to the sense of equilibrium which evolves between the different social actors in that setting. Generally people behave with some degree of regularity in a social setting, providing a feeling of reassurance to others, and a yardstick by which they can judge their own behaviour. In a school, for example, the staff know which colleagues arrive at work early. They also know which students arrive early, and which students are typically late. Some colleagues always perform administrative tasks promptly and others require several reminders. People tend to park their cars in the same places, and to make their cups of coffee at the same time. If you work in a college and are a course leader, you know the lecturers who will mark work and return it on time, and those who will delay until the last possible moment. You also usually know the students who will hand their assignments in on time, and those who will be always asking for extensions to the deadline. In short, although human interactions are never completely predictable, people do tend to develop patterns and consistencies in their behaviour.

Besides the routine aspects of life such as making cups of coffee, these consistencies also apply to our professional lives. As teaching colleagues get to know each other, they begin to learn the views and attitudes which others hold. They begin to be able to predict the views which people will take in meetings. They are able to some extent to predict the approach colleagues will take to new initiatives. If we are thinking of asking different colleagues if they would like to become involved in planning a new course, we may be able to predict their response with some degree of accuracy. All of these features contribute to the social ecology of the organizational setting.

Social ecology is never permanent, and is far from being totally predictable. As a form of equilibrium it is in a state of continual flux. All kinds of factors can change the equilibrium. If the management of a college decides to restructure the staffing organization, this is likely to affect the equilibrium considerably. Even if a single new member of the teaching staff is appointed, the arrival of that new colleague will affect the social ecology. Certainly, a group of researchers or even a single researcher conducting a research study in a school or college may have a significant effect upon the social setting.

A researcher may disturb the social ecology of a school primarily because the staff and students cannot quite understand the role occupied by the researcher. The latter is not a teacher, not a quality standards inspector, not a governor, not a parent, nor any other category of person who normally comes to the school. Both the staff and the students are aware that the researcher is gathering information, and that some of that information may come from them. They are aware that, to some extent, the manner in which they go about their daily lives will be subject to some scrutiny or observation. They assume that value judgements will be made about the way they do things, and this can lead to some level of anxiety. These feelings may be particularly relevant for the teaching staff, and may manifest themselves in a number of ways. Some teachers may be solicitous of the researcher, taking every opportunity to show examples of their teaching materials, and to invite the researcher into their classes. Others may be uncooperative and suspicious.

For a variety of reasons, some ethical and some concerned with the quality of the research data, it is desirable that the researcher disturbs the social ecology as little as possible. In research terms the researcher will probably want to collect data in as naturalistic a setting as possible. The less the school is disturbed by the research process the better. This will improve the validity of the research, in the sense that the data collected will more truly reflect the nature of the school as it really is, rather than having been amended by the research process. Equally well though, there is the ethical issue of the extent to which it is reasonable or fair to disturb the professional lives of teaching colleagues. There are many different positions one might adopt here. We might point out, as has already been argued, that there is no such thing as a completely stable social ecology, and hence the impact of a researcher will be no more significant than any other temporary visitor to the school. We could also adopt a form of consequentialist argument, in that we might argue that school-based research is designed to improve the quality of teaching and learning; although there may be some temporary impact on the school and teaching staff, this is justified by the long-term advantages. Nevertheless, there perhaps remains a feeling that whatever other justifications may be sought, it is unfair to disturb the professional lives of colleagues. Arguably, they are disturbed for all kinds of reasons, including quality inspections, and the intervention of researchers is simply adding to this burden.

There may be a compromise position. Teachers may find the impact of researchers intrusive and even stressful, especially when they do not fully understand the purpose and nature of their research. If this is so, perhaps the best strategy would be to try to inform the teachers and students about the research project as fully as possible, before the research commences. Informed consent may have been granted by the school governors and the headteacher, but it would arguably be unfair to expect that data could then be collected freely throughout the school. Before the research project started, it may be possible for the researcher to attend a staff meeting, and to explain the nature of the project to all the staff. Notices could be placed around the school explaining the research project to the students, and providing photographs and identities of the researchers who they will see in the school. It may be possible for the researchers to become involved in normal school life, as in the role of a participant observer. This may help to gain the confidence of the teachers and the researcher may feel less of an intruder, but someone who is contributing to the life of the school. One might argue that such measures are undermining the very naturalism which they are designed to maintain. There is a fine balance here, between the researcher's wish to avoid disturbing the social ecology, and the potential impact of the methods used to try to achieve that end.

Observational studies in a public setting

Research in a public setting is sometimes described as field research and sometimes as naturalistic research. A public setting is any social context to which members of the public routinely have access. Examples might include a railway station, a city centre, a large department store, a motorway, a public swimming pool, or parts of some educational institutions. Perhaps the most significant ethical problem when conducting research in such settings is the extent to which people are entitled to privacy. A related question is the establishment of a demarcation line between private and public settings.

Let us imagine an archetypical private setting, such as the board room of a large corporation. If we wished to conduct an ethnographic study of a meeting of the directors, we would expect to have to obtain the permission of those present, and to submit ourselves to detailed questioning on the purposes and likely dissemination of our research.

On the other hand, if we attended a public meeting to which people had been invited to listen to a marketing talk on a new product, this is a very different type of context. We might feel that we would be justified in keeping field notes, since the speaker had made a specific attempt to attract people to listen. In research terms, however, there may still remain a number of issues upon which to reflect. Even in a public meeting, it may not be entirely clear whether any type of data collection is appropriate, or whether only some may be ethically permissible. For instance, there may be ethical and indeed legal reasons why the taking of photographs or the use of a video camera might be inappropriate.

One of the basic dilemmas for the researcher who seeks to carry out naturalistic research is that ideally the setting should have complete ecological validity. In other words, the setting should be undisturbed by any extraneous event. Clearly, once the researcher asks the participants in the setting whether data can be collected, the ecological validity is compromised. If we momentarily set the ethical issues on one side, then from a purely research viewpoint, the naturalistic research with the greatest validity involves a setting where the participants do not realize that they are being observed. However, ethical concerns may well require that participants are informed that the researcher wishes to maintain observational records.

A key factor in evaluating the ethical issues in this type of situation is the types of data which the researcher envisages collecting. Arguably the central factor is whether the data-collection method would enable participants to be identified later. This may be particularly significant if the data are stored for any time, and another researcher is able to gain access to them. Field notes or other forms of written observation would not normally enable participants to be identified, since it would be easy to use fictional identifiers. However, any form of visual data would clearly not ensure anonymity. If there were any possibility that participants might be identified from the data, it would be prudent to take the advice of a research ethics committee before commencing the research.

Sometimes, when planning research in a public setting, the intention is to gather data on a particular social group. Such a group might consist of higher education students, school students, shoppers within a particular category, or motorists. It may also involve research being conducted in a particular area of a city. Whenever this is the case, it is worth considering the extent to which this particular community, has been involved in research before. Excessive research in a particular area of a city can have various consequences. Potential participants may become alienated from the research activity, and either refuse to cooperate, or provide only minimal data. Participants may become sensitized to being observed and may not act naturally. Alternatively, participants may become familiar with the types of questions asked by researchers and develop standard responses.

The study of social groups in a public setting thus raises a number of complicated ethical issues, particularly concerning the privacy of participants. Let us conclude this section by considering two case studies which create fairly typical ethical dilemmas (see Box 5.3).

Issues of privacy are involved in both studies. In the case of those soliciting money from the public, it could be argued that they have placed themselves in the public domain, and are deliberately seeking the attention of passers-by. To that degree one might argue that they have relinquished their right to privacy. Equally well, one could argue that there is no connection between the researchers and the observees, hence there is unlikely to be any way in which their identity could be disclosed in a research report. If we assume that the researchers are careful not to use descriptions which might identify people, the anonymity of the observees is almost certainly assured. On this basis one might argue that there is no requirement to inform the observees that they are being observed. On the other hand, one might wish to take the view that these are unfortunate members of society, and that most people would not wish to live this kind of life. Setting on one side the perhaps cynical view that some people may spend their money inappropriately, one

---

Box 5.3   Ethical dilemma: research in a public setting

Two groups of researchers are considering observational studies in different contexts. One group is planning a study of begging in a large inner city. They intend to observe people who are soliciting money, and to make detailed field notes on the length of time they spend in a location, the types of locations that are frequented, the techniques used to solicit money, and to make an estimate from observations of the amount of money collected within a period of time.

The second group plan a study of the various teaching techniques used by university lecturers while they are delivering formal university lectures. The researchers are all students and have legitimate grounds for access to a variety of lectures in different subjects. They plan to keep detailed observational notes, and to maintain a record of the time devoted to different teaching approaches. They plan to compare different lecturers in terms of time devoted to question and answer, formal delivery of subject matter, use of visual aids, informal discussion and the use of handouts.

---

might argue that one should try to extend every kind of consideration to people in such circumstances, and that this should include seeking their informed consent about the research.

In the case of the university lecturers, it seems at least a possibility that if they were informed about the research, they may well adapt their style of lecture delivery to what they assumed might be expected. In other words, this would be a threat to the naturalism of the research. On the other hand, as people familiar with research activity, they may resist the temptation to deliberately change their delivery. One might argue that as lecturers they are used to being on public view, and also the probability that students will discuss their performance in lectures. Hence, as they are by virtue of their jobs being observed anyway, one might feel that there is no specific requirement to inform them of the research. It may be slightly more difficult to ensure the anonymity of lecturers. If the identity of the researchers is recorded in the research report, it may be possible, under certain circumstances, to identify the lecturers. This may be an argument for seeking informed consent. A further consideration is that a university lecture theatre is not a public location in the same way as a street in a city centre. The lecture theatre is a public space, but only to a restricted group of people. One might feel that it does not necessarily correspond to what one normally means by a public setting.

In summary, the conducting of observational research in a public setting may apparently justify the waiving of privacy rights and of the need for informed consent. However, a more careful consideration of the relevant factors suggests that these situations are complex, and that both ethical and legal concerns may indicate that some level of agreement from participants may be required. (For a discussion of ethical issues in field research, see Shaffir and Stebbins 1991: 16.)

Privacy in relation to institutions and organizations

Institutions and organizations, just as much as individuals, may be participants in research projects. They also have rights in terms of privacy, and it would be unfair to assume, simply because one is collecting data from a large organization, that some privacy entitlements may be waived. In order to explore the rights of organizations, it may be useful initially to distinguish between public companies whose principal function may be seen as providing a public service, and private companies on the other hand, whose prime purpose is to generate profits for shareholders. The differences in purpose may generate different ethical imperatives, and perhaps different entitlements in terms of privacy.

The situation with a public company whose principal function would appear to be to provide a public service may appear to be different from that of a private, commercial corporation. At first sight, one might argue that such organizations should, in principle, be completely open and accessible to researchers, allowing them to view databases and other sources of information. Even if this were the broad philosophical position, there would presumably still be exceptions, including the confidentiality requirements to protect data on named individuals. The broad ethical position with an organization which exists in principle to further the public good is that it should, by that fact, be prepared to make its procedures open to public scrutiny. There should generally be an expectation that researchers should receive as much help and assistance as possible, commensurate with the protection of named individuals.

In the case of private companies they may have both moral and legal rights to keep details of new product designs secret, and not to participate in any research programme which might jeopardize the confidentiality of such information. They may have similar rights in terms of requiring employees not to release any information which has commercial sensitivity. Private companies may maintain a variety of databases, and if approached by a legitimate research team, it is to be hoped that they would do their best to cooperate in making as many data available as possible. Indeed such collaboration, if publicized, may be commercially advantageous to them. Nevertheless, researchers have to accept that commercial companies are often in a competitive situation, and that they may genuinely feel that to cooperate in a specific research project may be potentially disadvantageous to them.

The distinction between public and private organizations may not always be as clear as one might suppose. Private companies may invest in public organizations, creating situations which are even more complex ethically. Organizations such as colleges and universities, which previously have been seen as being almost entirely within the public sector, may now be corporate entities. As a more commercial culture pervades areas of life which previously were seen as being a public service, different value systems may evolve. It is important that researchers recognize that organizational cultures do evolve to reflect social, economic and political changes in society, and hence the response of organizations in terms of privacy and confidentiality issues will evolve also.

The storage of data

The fundamental difficulty with the storage of research data is that with the passage of time, it may be used for other research purposes, or non-researchers may gain access to it. Even though the original researcher who collected the data may have complied scrupulously with privacy requirements, there may be no guarantee that future users of the data will do so. It is therefore important that those who collect the data initially, and who store it, give careful thought to the uses to which it might be put. In any situation where data may be stored or archived it is desirable that peer review of the procedure takes place, and an appropriate ethics committee is consulted. Probably one of the most desirable elements in any storage procedure is that all individuals should be anonymized as effectively as possible. If data should be used for some other purpose, this then minimizes any adverse effects for individual respondents.

Generally speaking it is not necessary to store all of the raw data from a research study, once that study has been written up as a thesis or as a journal article. If the data are qualitative in nature, the norm is to use suitably anonymized extracts in the thesis to support the arguments and analysis, and not to make available the entire body of data, which is likely to be substantial in the case of a qualitative study. With quantitative data such as completed questionnaires, it is again the norm to present the summative analysis, and not to save all the primary data. It is often the custom to provide a copy of the uncompleted questionnaire in order to demonstrate the manner in which the data were collected. One might argue that there could be the necessity for another researcher to reanalyse the data in order to confirm the results, and that this is a justification for data storage. However, this could be achieved shortly after the first analysis, thus removing the necessity to store the data. It is possible for another researcher to replicate the research design and to collect more data in a comparable context. The archiving of data is thus something which should be contemplated only after careful thought, and after taking the advice of an appropriate peer review committee.

6 Differences in the research context

Cultural differences

The participants in a research study will never be a uniform group, even when the size of the group is small, and the participants have been carefully selected. The members of the research sample will almost certainly possess some factors in common, to correspond with the main variables for the research. However, there will also be many ways in which they differ. Not only will they differ between themselves, but also they will almost certainly differ in a number of ways from the researcher. The differences, both between participants themselves, and between participants and the researcher, may involve dimensions such as values and attitudes, social customs, religious beliefs, ethnicity, gender, language, employment patterns and education. Such cultural differences are an almost inescapable feature of the research process and raise a number of ethical issues in research.

The cultural background of individual respondents almost inevitably affects the way in which they respond to requests for data during research. An example of a cultural factor is level of education. One respondent may have received a university education, while another respondent may have no experience of education beyond high school. The former will have a fairly good understanding of the research process and what the researchers are trying to achieve, while the latter may find the whole procedure rather perplexing. During the research, if they are both asked about the same issue, it is important that they are both able to reflect their personal views as accurately as possible. This is an ethical issue in the sense that the research should be designed in such a way that each respondent is able fully to comprehend what is being asked, and also to articulate accurately their values and attitudes about the issue in question. In a similar vein, if there are significant cultural differences between the researcher and the participants, these may militate against the researcher making valid interpretations of the data provided by the participants.

Research in a social setting often involves identifying subcultures; the interaction between subcultures may be significant in determining the characteristics of that social setting. Membership of a subculture and allegiance to that social group may have an important effect upon the way in which social members and research participants view the world. It may also affect the manner in which they respond to research questions and provide data. School-based research, and in particular research on classroom interactions, may be affected by student subcultures. In the ethical dialogue in Box 6.1, two researchers are discussing some research they have recently started on the attitudes to school work of a group of 14-year-old high school students. They feel that they have begun to discern the presence of several subcultures in the class, and that membership of these subcultures is a significant factor in student attitudes. Moreover, the presence of a dominant subculture appears to be having a significant effect upon the attitudes of those students who do not necessarily belong to that subculture (see Box 6.1).

Let us suppose for the moment that the researchers are correct in their analysis of the subcultures in the classroom. Where do the ethical issues lie in this research study? First, the students (and particularly the boys) in the hard-working group do not appear to be able to give voice to their true attitudes. They appear to be under the influence of the dominant group of students. In effect, they are not acting autonomously. The second ethical issue is that of the effect the research questioning may have upon them. One researcher at least is worried that asking them in detail about the pressure they might feel under could exacerbate this issue for them.

One possible attempt to resolve this issue would be to discuss the existence of subcultures in the class with the teaching staff of the school. They might be able to offer practical advice on the extent to which some of the students are influenced by the dominant group. This might enable judgements to be made about the form any further interviewing should take.

It is worth noting in the context of school subcultures that the preceding discussion concerned subcultures within a single classroom. The school as a whole will typically embrace a variety of other subcultures. The dominant ethos of the school, and a feature which could legitimately be described as the dominant ideology of the whole school, is one linked to academic success. Perhaps more than anything else, the public reputation of the school rests upon the successful reinforcement of that culture. To that extent, the hard-working students in the class are, in a sense, members of the school's dominant culture. There may be other significant cultures in the school, such as a sporting culture and also a culture involved with successful social interaction, including interaction with the local community of the school. It may be possible for a student to be socially successful in the school by being a significant member of both an academic and a sporting subculture.

Cultural differences in the research context can manifest themselves in a

---

Box 6.1   Ethical dialogue: the effect of subcultures on research

---

A: I don't want to anticipate the outcome of this study, but it seems to me there are three main subcultures in this class. There is one group of students who are antagonistic to the values of the school, and do as little work as possible. There is another group of students who work hard, but who do this covertly, and pretend to accept the norms of the previous group. Finally, there is a smaller group of students who work hard, and who do this overtly. Is this your general feeling?

B: It is, and I would add a couple of things. The first group you mention is the dominant group. They exert a lot of power in the class. I would also divide your final group into two divisions. There is a group of girls who work hard, and who are tolerated, if not accepted, by the dominant group. On the other hand, the relatively small number of boys in this group suffer a degree of taunting by the dominant group.

A: We've obviously come to the same conclusion. My main problem so far is that when I talk to students in the third, hard-working group, the boys in particular are obviously very reluctant to discuss their views about studying. My hunch is that they are unduly influenced by the value system of the dominant group. They almost pretend that they are not interested in studying, and yet when you look at their work this is obviously not so.

B: OK, I accept that this may be so, but if they really were so influenced by the dominant group, why would they continue working hard? It is obvious that they do work hard, both at home and at school.

A: Well, maybe they are just caught in a situation of dissonance, where they continue to work hard, and know that they are doing so, but just do not want to admit it publicly or to people like us.

B: Perhaps we just need to explore this with more subtle questioning.

A: We can certainly try that, but I think we ought to be sensitive to the psychological situation these students are in. Some of them are having quite a hard time of it. They want to do well academically, and yet seem to be subject to quite strong pressure to do just the opposite. It's a form of bullying really, and I would not like to subject them to what they might feel is a bit of an interrogation. It is just difficult to know whether it is best to discuss these things in the open, or to let them make whatever response they feel is appropriate.

---

variety of ways. Social members may interact using different linguistic codes, employing those codes, at least partly, to reinforce their membership of a particular social group. From a research viewpoint, it is important that researchers appreciate that participants may view the world from a variety of different perspectives. These perspectives may reflect to some degree the subcultures to which they belong. The researcher should be aware that the subculture of respondents may influence the manner in which they provide data, and the content of those data.

Another way in which school students may not be able to reflect their true feelings in a research context is when they are unable to communicate with the researcher within the same cultural framework or linguistic code. This situation is exacerbated when the researcher is communicating exclusively within the dominant academic culture of the school, and the student has not acquired the skills to do so. This may involve a form of cultural deprivation on the part of the student, where the latter has not been sufficiently exposed, either in the home or elsewhere, to this type of communication style and value system. This is illustrated in the ethical dilemma described in Box 6.2.

Box 6.2   Ethical dilemma: cultural deprivation

In a study of the aspirations of final year high school students to attend college and university, the researcher is concerned that a number of students do not appear to have an understanding of what is entailed by higher education. They do not appear to understand the nature of a degree course or the types of activities which it typically involves. Nor do they appear to appreciate the education or pragmatic advantages of a period of such study. Some students, on the other hand, appear to have a varying degree of understanding, gained either from older siblings, or from what they have been told by parents. The researcher is concerned that questions on aspirations towards higher education may have limited meaning and significance for students who have not gained any appreciation of the nature of university study.

The main ethical issue here is that some students do not appear to have an adequate cultural background to enable them to respond to the questions about higher education. One might argue that the researcher should explore techniques which might enable all students to respond in some way. One strategy might be to provide a short video film and talk on the experience of higher education to all students. This might not ensure that students all had the same knowledge base from which to answer questions, but should help most students to have at least something to say in response to the research questions.

However, there is a different perspective on this issue. Both this dilemma and the previous ethical dialogue raise the question of whether the researcher ought to try to amend a situation where some respondents are better able to respond to research questions than others. One might wish to argue that there is a certain inevitability about some participants being better informed than others, at responding to research questions. Further, one could argue that one should not try to change such a situation, but rather accept it for the way it is. This type of issue illustrates the debate in ethics between naturalistic theories and non-naturalistic theories (see Box 6.3).

Box 6.3   Theoretical perspective: naturalistic and non-naturalistic theories of ethics

The distinction between these two types of theories centres upon the issue of whether it is possible to deduce ethical propositions from empirical statements. For example, one might start from the empirical observation that a student has failed to hand in an important piece of homework. The teacher may deduce from this that the student ought to be punished. In other words, a moral judgement has been developed from an empirical statement. Naturalists would support the idea that such an argument was possible. Non-naturalists, on the other hand, would argue that there is no logical way in which moral statements may be deduced from empirical statements. The philosopher G.E. Moore famously described the attempt to deduce moral statements from non-moral ones as 'naturalistic fallacy'. He summarized it as the attempt to derive an 'ought' from an 'is' (see Frankena 1967: 50–63).

Hence one could argue that in any sample of research participants, there will normally be individuals who are representative of different subcultures. If so, this is a matter which is subject to empirical verification. One might then argue that the participants should be provided with such information, to help them all be able to respond in some way to the research questions. This proposition adopts a value position and, as it stands, is an attempt to argue an ethical statement from an empirical one. Whether or not this is perceived as justifiable, depends at least partly upon whether you accept the argument of the naturalists or non-naturalists.

Gender differences

Gender is often treated as a variable in research designs and questionnaires will typically include a question to establish the gender of the respondent. In survey research involving the use of questionnaires, gender is often regarded as a causal or independent variable. In other words, fluctuations in a different variable are investigated in order to explore whether these changes may be affected by gender differences. A typical investigation might involve examining student scores in a mathematics test, in order to ascertain whether there were significant differences between male and female students.

However, whether or not gender is treated as a specific causal variable, it remains a significant determinant of the way in which respondents provide data, and in which researchers interpret data. Gender remains one of those characteristics of the human condition, along with social class, age and ethnicity, which contribute greatly to the particular way in which we view the world. An older person does not look out at the world in quite the same way as a teenager. It is extremely difficult to shed the combined social experiences of a number of decades, and view the world in exactly the way one did when younger. In an analogous way it is important for social researchers to appreciate the diverse and subtle ways in which human beings are progressively socialized into belonging to a particular gender. Almost from the very point of birth, individuals are conditioned into understanding and conceptualizing the world as a member of a gender group. This socializing process affects the way in which they interact with members of the same gender, members of the opposite gender, and generally the way in which they understand the world. Through gender are transmitted value systems and norms of behaviour. This is not to assume that there is one set of norms of behaviour characteristic of each gender. What it means to be a male or a female may differ considerably from one social culture to another; this is not to refer to the culture in one country or another, since gender-related value systems may vary enormously from house to house on the same street in the same town.

As researchers it is important to remind ourselves of the all-embracing manner in which the social world is gendered. When a research respondent is asked a question, they will perceive the question and respond to it, partly at least, as a member of a gender group. If we ask people what they think of the state of health provision in the country, they will analyse that question at least partly as a male or as a female. That analysis will almost certainly focus to a considerable extent upon their own health concerns, and the extent to which they feel those are likely to be met by current health provision.

However, it is not always easy for any individual to distinguish between a gendered analysis of a situation, and an analysis which is gender-neutral. It is possible for the gendered socialization process to make it difficult to recognize when we are analysing an issue from a gendered viewpoint! Consider the ethical dilemma described in Box 6.4.

The ethical dilemma here is a variant of the issue of data validity. It is a question of trying as much as possible, to ensure that the data provided by respondents accurately reflect their views, or alternatively, that the researcher does not make unwarranted and unnecessary assumptions. Let us assume that the male headteacher in Box 6.4 actually is very assertive with the students. There could be a variety of explanations for this. First, the headteacher as a person could simply have inherited an assertive personality. Second, the headteacher could have been socialized as a child into a culture of male assertiveness and even aggression. Third, the headteacher may be responding to his perception of the expectations of the students in terms of male

---

Box 6.4 Ethical dilemma: gendered analysis

Two researchers, a woman and a man, are conducting research into the gendered nature of the high school headteacher role. They intend to interview a sample of female headteachers and male headteachers to explore the extent to which the post-holders are aware of the gendered nature of their roles. The researchers decide that it might be better if the male researcher interviews the female headteachers and the female researcher the male headteachers. They feel that this might help a sense of ethnographic strangeness being retained in the research situation. In other words, they feel that it may minimize any taken-for-granted assumptions being made by the researchers, if both interviewer and interviewee were of the same gender. The researchers are concerned whether they should specifically ask questions about gendered roles. If, for example, they were to ask a male headteacher whether he felt he had to appear assertive and even aggressive at times, in order to comply with the role expectations of the male students, that the question might implicitly suggest a particular answer. They wondered whether it might be a better strategy to try to infer gendered views directly from the data provided in response to other questions.

---

behaviour. There may be other possibilities! The problem for the researcher is to try to ascertain the extent to which respondents are aware of these possibilities, and the extent to which they are able to analyse their own social responses.

The dilemma for the researchers is that if they ask a question which is too focused, they may be inviting a particular response from the headteachers. On the other hand, if they ask a more general question, it may be so undirected that the headteachers do not really appreciate the nature of the issue which they are raising.

A separate but related issue is that the extent to which individuals reflect upon the gendered nature of their work roles may be related to the number of their gender occupying such roles. For example, there are generally fewer female high school headteachers or principals than male headteachers. Males may thus conceptualize themselves as headteachers rather than male headteachers. Females may be much more aware of the nature of their gender in relation to their role, and hence may conceptualize themselves as female headteachers. The latter may be sensitive to the kinds of distinctive features which they as women can bring to the job, and to such issues as the ways in which they are perceived by staff and students.

If this analysis is correct, it may be that females in some roles in education may prefer certain types of inquiry methods to others. If they wish to be more reflective about the gendered nature of their role, then qualitative, interpretative methods may give them greater opportunities to analyse this aspect of their role. The self-completion questionnaire, with its tendency for precisely defined, focused questions may not give such opportunities. Males, on the other hand, may be satisfied to provide data in a more focused, less reflective form. Such a distinction may be appropriate in many cases, but, of course, is not generally applicable.

Differences of ethnicity

Ethnicity is a complex characteristic of people, and in a research context raises sophisticated issues. The difficulties start perhaps with gaining an adequate appreciation of the concept of ethnicity, and a working definition which enables researchers to treat it as a variable in a research study. Before considering ethical issues, let us analyse some features of the concept of ethnicity.

The relatively recent increase in use of the term is linked with dissatisfaction with the use of the term 'race' (see Fenton 1999: 66). The latter has become regarded as rather unsatisfactory through the difficulties inherent in defining human 'races' in the same way in which the term is used broadly in biological studies. Once it became clear that the genetic basis of the term in the context of human beings was problematic (Eriksen 1997: 34), there was a need for another term such as ethnicity. This term, while avoiding some of the unfortunate connotations of 'race', nevertheless embraces different elements of social culture and history, and for an adequate understanding requires considerable analysis.

Perhaps the most important element of ethnicity is that it is a characterizing term which is founded in the social life of groups of people. It is also an evolving characteristic. In other words, the elements which make up ethnicity do not necessarily remain the same, but are revised and revised again by the members of an ethnic group. For example, the history of a group of people may consist of certain historical 'facts' such as wars and migrations, but the understanding of those events may change. The way in which they are interpreted, and used to interpret the contemporary world, may alter a number of times.

Migrants from the Indian subcontinent to the United Kingdom since the Second World War experienced a number of major changes in British society which have had an impact upon subsequent generations. The migrant generation and subsequent generations also have had different experiences of their own ethnic background. The migrant generation may well have lived through the realities of the partition of the subcontinent into India and Pakistan, while this is merely a historical event to the descendants of these original migrants. In addition, the original migrant generation had experience of living in the subcontinent with a very different lifestyle from that in Britain.

Ethnicity is related to religious customs, to a moral belief system, and to political beliefs. It is also linked to the economic experiences of a group of people. Early migrants from the Indian subcontinent were understandably concerned with establishing themselves economically, and with obtaining suitable housing. The early realities of life tended to consist of working in jobs which were regarded generally as less desirable by the indigenous population, and living in poorer quality urban housing. Thus the early experiences of these migrant groups were frequently ones involving urban deprivation, which could be considered as becoming part of the ethnicity of a number of groups.

Language is a central element in ethnicity, since it is through language that the key elements of ethnic identity are conveyed within the group, frequently along with such cohesive factors as religious scriptures and an understanding of historical events. Language and education frequently combine in sustaining an ethnic identity, and it is noticeable and understandable how ethnic groups from the Indian subcontinent have given considerable attention to attempts to encourage and sustain a competence in their own languages among the younger generations.

Language is an important element in research, since it is the medium through which data are provided and then analysed. It is also the medium through which an ethnic group conveys complex conceptual ideas which may be a distinctive feature of its own ethnicity. In research in a multiethnic community, where respondents may have different ethnic backgrounds, it is important that the researchers decide on a policy with regard to language. In a research study in which a team of researchers are investigating racial discrimination in employment in an inner-city, multiethnic community, the research team are unsure how to cope with the variety of languages among potential respondents. A variety of Asian languages are spoken in the community, and many members of the community speak only very limited English. Two researchers discuss the issue in Box 6.5.

Where there are language variations in the research population, it is important that respondents have the opportunity to express their true feelings, particularly about an issue as important as discrimination. The ideas and feelings which they wish to convey may be very complex and subtle, and they may be realistically conveyed only in their mother tongue. In terms of a research area involving the potential unfair treatment of people, there is an ethical issue that all respondents should have the opportunity to explain their personal experiences of the issue, and articulate the ways in which they feel the situation could be improved.

It is important that a mechanism be found to ensure that all respondents give their informed consent to take part in the research. This process clearly involves the research participants in understanding exactly what is involved in the research, and it is difficult to facilitate this process where there are any

---

Box 6.5 Ethical dialogue: language issues in research

A: We could just recruit participants for the sample who spoke fluent English. It would not be difficult to find sufficient respondents.

B: There would be advantages to that. It would be easier for us to discuss the issues we were interested in, but it would be a very biased sample. I suspect most of the respondents would be younger people.

A: That's probably true. It depends whether the advantages outweigh the disadvantages. I think really we ought to decide on our criteria for recruiting respondents, primarily in relation to the issue of employment. After all, that is the issue we are investigating. Some of those may speak little English, and we will just have to deal with that.

B: OK, so what will be our strategy? We could use interpreters; we could employ research assistants to go out into the community and collect the data for us; or we could try to make ourselves understood in a limited way.

A: I quite like the idea of research assistants from the ethnic minority groups. The advantage of that idea is that they could interview both the English speakers and the non-English speakers alike. This should give some sort of consistency to the process. They could even use the mother tongue language throughout, even with those who speak English.

B: Yes, then any conceptual misunderstandings would be possibly more evenly distributed.

A: If we gave the research assistants a good induction to the research process, it could be the most consistent method of collecting data, and improve the validity.

B: They might also give us useful advice about ways of asking questions to explore employment discrimination.

---

language differences between the researcher and respondent. It may be easier to convey the required information to a bilingual third party who can then communicate clearly with the respondents in their mother tongue.

Religious differences

When conducting research in the industrialized 'West' it is easy to forget the impact which religious belief can have on the worldviews of some groups. In many parts of North America and Europe it is some considerable time since there was a widespread integration of religious belief and the broad culture of society. This is generally not the case in Islamic societies, with regard to Hindus and Sikhs in India, and in a number of Buddhist societies. In such cases, religious practices and beliefs have a significant effect on daily life and in particular on the kind of worldview or general philosophy of life to which individual people adhere.

In the West, when we are collecting research data from respondents of a range of religious beliefs, it is important to remember that the religious belief may have an impact upon the way the particular data-collection instrument is viewed. Issues about the nature of valid knowledge, the nature of that which is morally acceptable, and questions about that which is acceptable in society, may all be affected by religious belief. When conducting research in a multi-ethnic and multi-religious society it is almost inevitable that religion will in effect be a research variable. In a multi-religious area, any random sampling procedure will almost certainly result in a multi-religious sample. Only in a purposive sample where the researcher embarked on the process of selecting a sample composed of just one religious group, would this not be so. Let us now look briefly at some of the features of conducting research in multi-religious societies, which may have implications for research ethics.

Although it may be platitudinous to say so, it is important to indicate that different religions have different ethical perspectives. As research is often concerned with values, attitudes and judgements about variables, it is reasonable to assume that religious factors will affect the kinds of responses which are given. More than that, it is worth remembering that many religious groups make special efforts to sustain an understanding of religious history and belief among the younger generations. Whether it is lessons in an understanding of the Qur'ān at a mosque, or lessons on the Panjabi language and Sikh religion at the gurdwara, many religious communities take a great pride in sustaining an understanding of religious belief and practice. (The provision of education for Hindu children is discussed in Jackson and Nesbitt 1993: 147–65.) This religious belief has a pivotal role in maintaining a sense of the collectivity in many ethnic minority communities.

This leads us to a different issue, which is important in research terms, and which is clearly an ethical issue. This is the question of the descriptors which are employed for different religious and ethnic groups. In the case of religious groups which trace their ethnicity to the Indian subcontinent, a variety of descriptors are used including Asian, Indian, Pakistani or Bangladeshi. A descriptor is important because it gives an indication of the ethnicity of the people involved, and as such is a statement about the individuals who constitute that ethnic group. Moreover, descriptors should focus upon the features of that ethnic group which are central to its identity. The descriptor 'Asian' seems inadequate through its very generality, unless the research is comparing participants from entire continents. It would certainly be inadequate in any research which was focusing upon country of origin or of religion, because it embraces far too large an area, and too great a sense of potential diversity. The other three descriptors mentioned would be satisfactory in any research project which focused upon country of origin as being a significant variable. In the case of religion as a variable, Pakistan and Bangladesh, as predominantly Muslim countries, would be satisfactory descriptors. India, on the other hand, embraces a diversity of religious belief, including Hinduism, Sikhism, Islam, Zoroastrianism, Jainism and Christianity. Even within Hinduism, there are many variations and subcultures in different parts of India. It may therefore be more appropriate, and indeed important in research terms, to describe someone as a Hindu from rural Bihar, or a Hindu from central Bombay. The fundamental requirement of any descriptor is that it is sufficiently precise to be fair to the individual people to whom it is allocated, and also of relevance to the variables which form the general approach of the research.

Ethical systems vary between religions, and these may have a significant effect on the approaches of research respondents. It is difficult and in some ways unsatisfactory to generalize in terms of religions, but there would probably be some justification in arguing that religions of the Judaeo-Christian tradition tend to be rather more absolutist in terms of ethics, than those which evolved within the Indian tradition. The Judaeo-Christian tradition probably tends to emphasize codes of ethical conduct which it is argued should be applied to a variety of everyday circumstances. There is an attempt to define good and evil in fairly strict terms, and to expect adherence to such moral codes from members of the faith. Such codes of conduct are normally seen as having been derived from the Divine.

The Indian tradition of Hinduism and Buddhism is perhaps more relativistic. Although there are ethical codes, such as parts of the Noble Eight-fold Path in Buddhism, these often take the form of general expressions of what is desirable. There is much less a sense of 'sin', since if a person acts in an unethical way, it is seen as something which will inevitably affect life in any future existence. In other words, it is seen in a much more personal way. It is viewed rather less as an infringement of a divine command, and more as an act which through karma and rebirth will have consequences for any future existence of the individual. Although this is a simplistic distinction, it does indicate a difference in ethical perspective, which inevitably will have an effect on the perception of research issues.

Where gender, religion and ethnicity are combined as variables in a research population, further complexities may arise. In the case of gender, it may be more reasonable to speak of the situation with regard to Asian women, rather than that of women in some of the different religions mentioned above. Thus, with a considerable caution about the difficulties of generalizing, it may be useful to make some tentative suggestions about the interaction of gender with religion and ethnicity, and the possible impact upon research. Although it may be argued that there is a difference in the social role of women in say the Parsi community of Bombay, compared with the social role of women in rural Pakistan, nevertheless, it is possible to make some broad suggestions about the role of women in Indian and Asian society.

There is a form of dichotomy between the theoretical social position of women in terms of religion, and that status which is accorded to women in a practical sense. Religion may sometimes suggest that women be treated in an egalitarian manner which seems somewhat removed from the actuality of life in rural Asia. Quite apart from the impact of religion, other variables such as social class clearly have a major impact upon the status of women. It is therefore possible in a research programme in the United Kingdom that Asian women respondents may find it an unusual experience to be asked questions about their thoughts and attitudes. As discussed, much might depend upon whether they had lived in a city environment or in a rural environment, and on the nature of any employment experience.

Differences of religion among respondents may create both an interesting research context, and also one involving a variety of possible ethical issues.

The collection of data when the researcher is of a different culture or gender from that of respondents

It may frequently be the case that there is a gender difference between researcher and respondents, and in a multiethnic society, there may be differences of religion, ethnicity and culture. Let us consider a case study of two English researchers who are collecting data on the Hindu community in a large English city. One of the researchers receives an invitation from an Indian undergraduate at the local university to visit his grandfather at his home. The undergraduate explains that his grandfather has lived on his own since his wife died, and that he is always happy to receive visitors. Although he does not speak any English, the student offers to accompany the researcher and to act as interpreter. After the visit, the researcher explains to a colleague what happened on the visit, and they discuss ethical issues which had arisen (see Box 6.6).

One gets the impression here, rightly or wrongly, that the grandfather has tried to transpose the culture within which he grew up in India to the United Kingdom. He appears to have surrounded himself with a culture and way of life which have a great deal of significance for him. The researcher has a strong sense of the meeting of two cultures, and does not wish to have any adverse impact upon the life of the grandfather. It is at least questionable whether, in such a situation, a formal attempt at informed consent would really be meaningful. Probably if Kumar at least mentioned that the researcher was trying to find out about Hinduism, then that would be sufficient. There was probably a sense in which the visit was enriching for the grandfather, and this in itself is an ethical dimension of the research. He enjoyed showing his garden to the researcher, and arguably in such situations there is an interface between research and a useful social function.

Box 6.6   Ethical dialogue: fieldwork in cross-cultural research

---

A: Well, I went with Kumar to his grandfather's house. It was mid-morning and I got the impression that he would normally have gone to the temple by then. It is about a mile and a half away, and he always walks it several times a day. I think the older Hindus use it as a sort of social centre. They meet and chat, and they can make a drink there. When we went in, he was very nice to me. He's obviously very literate, and reads a lot of mainly religious books. He made Kumar and me a drink of milky tea, which he brewed up in a saucepan in the kitchen. It was sweet and spicy – very nice. We sat in the living room and he took a book down off the bookshelf. Kumar said it was the *Bhagavadgītā*. The grandfather held the book and turned to me and said 'God – very good!' We nodded and smiled at each other. On a shelf across the room was a kind of small shrine. There were small statues, joss sticks, and lots of gold trimmings and decoration. He told me through Kumar that he got up in the morning and said prayers to God, and then made food offerings at the shrine. He then set off to walk to the Hindu temple. He seems to meet people there, but I think he leads a fairly monastic existence. He said he wanted to show me his vegetable garden. We went out to the back of the house, and he had this really well-prepared garden. He showed me his spinach, which he obviously grows a lot. While he was showing me this, he thumped his chest hard, and said 'Strong!Strong!' Kumar said that he put spinach in a lot of his food, because he felt it was very good for his health.

B: The visit seems to have gone well.

A: It did. He said we could both go back any time. I had a real sense though of being in a different culture. It was just an ordinary house from the outside, but once inside I might have been a thousand miles away.

B: What do you mean exactly?

A: Well, he was part of a completely different culture. And being older, I think that culture was deeply rooted in him. Kumar understood it, but was not totally a part of it either. I think the grandfather was basically happy in his world, and I didn't want to disturb him. Everything in that house meant a lot to him, and I did not want to do anything which was inappropriate.

B: Do you think he enjoyed you going?

A: Oh, I think so. I don't think he gets many visitors, so it was good from that point of view. I felt I had to be careful not to raise any issues which might concern him.

B: Like what?

A: Well, perhaps experiences of discrimination, say. I wouldn't have wanted to stir up perhaps unpleasant memories.

This case study concerns a situation where the researcher is of a different religion and ethnicity from that of the respondent. There is another way in which there may be a difference of culture between researcher and respondent and that is as a result of educational and social class differences. Researchers are usually well-educated people who are familiar with expressing themselves in quite sophisticated language, using complex ideas and concepts. Although some research involves collecting data from equally well-educated people, this is far from necessarily so. Although there may not always be a close connection between level of educational attainment, social class and economic status, in some cases researchers may exhibit differences of social class and economic status from the respondents. This may result in the researcher and the respondent finding it rather difficult to relate to each other. There may be a difficulty of communication arising through the use of rather formal language by the researcher, or lack of communication may arise through the use of colloquial language by some respondents. Research participants may find it difficult to understand the purpose of the research, and hence may be less able to make appropriate responses to questions. Some respondents may be intimidated to some extent by the research situation. They may view the researcher as representative of a large official organization such as a university, and may feel it is rather daunting to be asked questions by an academic.

From an ethical point of view it is important that as far as possible the respondent does not feel intimidated by the research process. Attempts should be made to speak to them in a friendly, reassuring manner, and in a location where they are likely to feel at ease. They could be asked relatively straight-forward questions initially, to give them confidence, followed by questions on the more complex issues. It is possible that some respondents may perceive the research process as a kind of 'test' which is endeavouring to find out how much they know about something. They should be reassured as much as possible that this is not at all the purpose, and that the research is interested only in their views, attitudes and experiences of the topic in question.

When the researcher is of a different culture from that of the respondents, it is important that neither the data-collection instrument nor the general dialogue between researcher and respondent indicate any view which holds the respondent's culture to be less significant in any way from that of the researcher. The question of the comparative value of different cultures is a complex issue concerned with the nature of a multicultural or multiethnic society, and also that of ethnocentrism.

The question of a multicultural society raises the issue of the equality of different cultures and societies. For some it may be part of the concept of multiculturalism and of multiethnicity, that different cultures are in fact of equal worth. However, it is fairly easy to imagine a theoretical society in which the social systems are so undesirable that one would never want to live there. We would surely not wish to live in a society where the powerful used the populace as a source of slave labour; where those accused of minor crimes were tortured; and where long terms of imprisonment awaited those who uttered any criticism of the ruling elite. We may then think of some actual cultures and societies, either historically or in the present day, in which some or all of these characteristics pertained. We may then agree that all societies are not equal, at least in the sense that all of their customs are not as apparently desirable as each other.

However, much depends on what we mean by the equality of cultures. We may choose to interpret the word 'equality' as indicating that all cultures are deserving of equal consideration in terms of their worth and value. In other words, we do not automatically reject a culture or society as being inferior, without giving it due consideration and applying certain carefully evaluated criteria. We may then decide that according to certain criteria, and according to our application of them, one society is preferable to another. This perhaps allows that someone may argue that the criteria themselves are socially con-structed, and hence that we cannot claim that they have absolute applicability and relevance. According to this argument, one person may rank several societies in one order, and another person may rank them in another order. However, there still remains the sense in which cultures are equal, in that all cultures are evaluated using rational criteria. They are perhaps treated equally in the process of their evaluation, using rationally derived criteria, rather than being ultimately regarded as equal. There remains a further debate about the nature of the criteria which might be used to compare cultures, but it is at least an important element of multiculturalism that members of one society do not make unwarranted assumptions about the qualities of another society. It is possible for members of one society to become so familiar with thinking about the world from their own cultural perspective, that they do not recognize the existence of alternative world views. Such a situation is that described by the term ethnocentrism.

It is almost inevitable that all cultures are ethnocentric to some extent. Each member of a society tends to use the conceptual framework of that society in terms of norms, values, customs and other elements of what we normally refer to as 'culture'. This may result in their viewing the same issue in a different way from a member of a different culture. While one may look at an issue from one's own cultural viewpoint, it is still logically possible to recognize that there are alternative views, and indeed to recognize that these views may have their own virtues. However, if one is operating from an ethno-centric perspective, one may simply not recognize that there are alternative worldviews and perspectives. Equally, one might acknowledge that there are other ways of looking at the world, but may in fact reject these perspectives as in some way less appropriate or unsuitable. Ethnocentrism as a concept is often of particular significance where there is a culture which is dominant in say economic and political terms, and has a tendency not to recognize the value of other cultures. At various points in history, there has arguably been a tendency for European cultures not always to recognize the value of other cultures, particularly when they did not have the same level of technological development as Europe. Such a view is sometimes described as Eurocentric.

It is important to be conscious of the possibility of implicit ethnocentrism, when the researcher is of a different culture to that of the respondents. In the next case study, two British researchers are conducting comparative research on teaching and learning styles in Britain and in several southern African countries. They conduct some preliminary interviews with African students studying in Britain, prior to a visit to southern Africa. They discuss some of the difficulties which arose during the interviews (see Box 6.7).

Box 6.7   Ethical dialogue: ethnocentrism in research

A: I thought the interviews went well, but there clearly are differences in terms of the style of teaching.

B: You mean when the African students were talking about our ideas of student-centred learning and independent learning.

A: That's right. They generally seem to prefer to have lectures and to be given information.

B: That does seem to be what they are saying to us so far. However, I don't want to make too many early assumptions. Also I want to be very careful about giving the impression that we think our teaching and learning approaches are better. I don't want them to feel at all that we are trying to persuade them to use student-centred approaches.

A: No, of course not. After all, we use didactic approaches at times. It is just a matter of emphasis.

B: I think we should perhaps try to avoid any sense of comparing the different teaching methods in use, because we could easily find ourselves in a position of implying that some methods are better than others. If we take the line that to some extent, teaching and learning styles can be related to the wider expectations of the particular society, and to the prevalent culture, we should be able to avoid that.

A: I more or less agree. I think inevitably we will have to compare different methods, and what they can achieve, but I agree that we can explore the extent to which they are context dependent and culture dependent.

Researchers can easily give the impression to respondents that the learning methods they use personally, or the methods with which they are familiar in their own educational system, are the more desirable. It is easy to treat the current practices in Europe or North America as if they represent a form of received wisdom which the rest of the world should emulate. To adopt such a stance would generally be a form of ethnocentrism. It may be better to consider the advantages and disadvantages of different learning styles, and then, as the researchers suggest, to discuss the social context within which one learning style is seen as more appropriate than another. The debate becomes less a question of trying to place different methods in a rank order.

A related issue occurs where the researcher wishes to treat ethnicity or cultural background as a variable, and selects a research sample composed of different ethnic groups. Some or all of these groups may have a different ethnicity or culture from that of the researcher. The major methodological issue is to determine a procedure for placing potential respondents into a particular ethnic category. This issue is similar, in many ways, to that of ethnic monitoring, whereby governments or other official agencies try to determine the numbers of different ethnic groups in the population.

In research terms, the researcher may have determined the overall research population, and know that this population contains individuals representing a variety of different ethnic groups. However, it is problematic for the researcher to attempt to place people in different groups, since the affiliations which people possess, and the way in which they perceive their own ethnicity, may differ considerably. The most appropriate technique may well be to use a system of self-allocation. The participants are provided with a list of ethnic categories and asked to allocate themselves to the category which they feel is most appropriate. It is usually necessary to include a fairly large number of categories, since it is important to meet the self-definitions of as many people as possible. The alternative strategy is to ask individuals to define and name categories themselves. The difficulty with this approach is that the result may be a very large number of categories, which then require reclassification. However, the fundamental ethical issue here is arguably that participants should have the right to place themselves within the ethnic grouping of their choice. The categorization should not be externally imposed by the researcher, because it is virtually impossible for a researcher to fully comprehend the basis upon which an individual conceptualizes their own culture and ethnicity. There are so many complex variables which contribute to our understanding of our own ethnicity, that any external classification will almost inevitably make assumptions, some of which are likely to be incorrect.

Perhaps to put this in a slightly different way, the manner in which people think of their ethnicity is connected with such concepts as personal freedom, autonomy and self-determination. Acknowledging that research participants should have the freedom to define their own ethnicity is arguably connected with respect for persons, which is a central element of the ethics of research. Ultimately, the way in which the research sample is defined can have an important effect upon the validity of the research data; perhaps more importantly, the procedures which are used should give participants the confidence that researchers are sensitive to the way in which they choose to define their own place in society.

Differences of gender between the researcher and respondent may sometimes create the necessity for special consideration during the data-collection process. This may be especially so where the researcher is male and the respondent female, because the researcher is inevitably cast in a role where there is a varying element of power and authority. The researcher is the person with a detailed knowledge of the research programme, and it is the researcher who has organized the research setting and who is asking the questions. The gender-related elements of such a situation become even more significant where the researcher has an employment-related position of authority over the respondent, for example, if the researcher is a college head of department and the respondent is a lecturer in that department. The fundamental ethical issue is that there should be an atmosphere of equality between the researcher and respondent. Respondents should not feel that because of any element of the research situation, nor because of any influence brought to bear by the researcher, that they have to answer questions or to continue with the research process when otherwise they might have felt inclined to end the data collection. To put this another way, the researcher should not seek to exercise any control or influence over the respondent, nor in fact, should be able to exercise such influence. It is the responsibility of the researcher to structure the research situation in such a way that the exercise of any control or influence is very improbable.

The location of the data collection is important. Particularly in the case of interview research it is preferable if the interview takes place in a room, the interior of which may be seen by people outside: the room should ideally have a glass-fronted door or a window looking out onto a corridor. The interview may then take place in a private and quiet environment, but also in a sense within the public domain. It may be preferable if the respondent sits nearer the door than the interviewer. These measures help to create a context in which the respondent may feel that they can terminate the interview at any time. There should also be no height difference between the chairs occupied by the interviewer and the respondent. If the interviewer's chair were higher, this would simply reinforce any impression of the interviewer occupying a role of authority in the situation.

There may be situations where it is undesirable for a male researcher to interview a female respondent, even given the circumstances described previously. In some Asian cultures for example, it is inappropriate for women to be in the company of men who are beyond the immediate family. When there is any possibility that this may be the situation, the researcher should take advice from members of that cultural community, in order to ascertain what might be an appropriate arrangement for the research. One possibility is that a female researcher is briefed on the details of the inquiry, and then conducts the interview. Another possibility is that there is another female of the interviewee's choosing present during the interview. Although these amendments to procedure do make it difficult to standardize the data-collection process, it is important that the respondents feel comfortable about the research process. Indeed, it is a theme of research ethics which has been reiterated at various times in this discussion that the respondent should not feel ill at ease during the research process, and that every attempt should be made to create a reassuring and supportive environment.

Issues specific to research in a health or social care context

There are features of the process of conducting research in a health or social care context which are somewhat different from other situations. While they raise the same broad ethical principles, the context of the research participants is undoubtedly different. The principal difference arises because the research participants are usually in a situation in which they are receiving care. In a health context the participants may be receiving treatment for physical or psychological illness, while in a social care context, participants may be receiving care, guidance or assistance for a variety of factors in their life. The latter might include addiction, substance abuse, homelessness, family violence, separation or divorce, children truanting from school, or unemployment. Some of the individuals who find themselves in such a health or social care context may be characterized by not being able to function normally in society. Illness may prevent people from carrying out some of their normal activities, and some of the examples of social care contexts listed earlier may prevent people from functioning as they might wish in society.

In one sense, such people have a great deal to contribute in research terms. Through their situation they often have a unique insight into certain social conditions, and can provide data which can be useful to social planners. They can provide charitable organizations or government agencies with the kinds of personal data which help them to appreciate the social circumstances under which many fellow human beings have to exist. However, these people are often in unenviable circumstances. They may be suffering in a variety of ways, either from physical pain if ill, or from physical discomfort if living in adverse circumstances. Importantly, they may also be suffering psychologically from the consequences of feelings of failure in life. This might apply to a person who is having great difficulty finding a permanent home. No matter how they might be conscious of the circumstances which have led up to their situation, and perhaps to many of these circumstances being outside their control, they may still suffer from feelings of inadequacy.

The essential ethical dilemma is whether it is morally acceptable to approach people who are ill or who are living in adverse circumstances, and ask them to help with a research programme. Part of the problem is that people react to circumstances in different ways. While some people may welcome the opportunity to discuss their difficulties, and perhaps find it helpful, others may prefer to keep their problems to themselves. One cannot generalize in such situations and develop a strategy that will be suitable for all people.

An important variable in such circumstances is the nature of the research. If a patient is suffering from a rare condition, and a specialist in that area asks if the patient would assist with some research, the patient may feel inclined to help on the grounds that it would be difficult for the researcher to find an alternative source of data, and that the research may help future sufferers. On the other hand, if the same patient was approached by a researcher investigating aspects of the hospital catering service, the patient might feel that this is an unnecessary intrusion. Different kinds of research will be perceived by people as having more or less significance and value. This assessment of the research will be an important factor in determining their willingness to be a participant in the research.

Not only will potential participants make judgements about being involved in the data collection, but also the researcher's peers and fellow professionals have an important role to play in forming judgements about the ethical probity of proposed research. They may make these judgements in an informal way, or they may be determined within the more formal confines of an ethics committee. Where it is the intention to collect data from hospital patients, it will normally be necessary to have the research proposal approved by the relevant ethics committee. With regard to research where the participants are in receipt of formal social care, there will normally be a procedure for ethics approval. It can also be helpful and instructive to consult colleagues informally, in order to obtain advice, before proceeding to, say, an ethics committee.

The identification of a research sample may be far from easy in the case of people who are receiving social care. Issues of the confidentiality of data may preclude professionals from divulging the names of people who are in a certain category of social care. Hence it may not be possible for the researcher to identify a random sample in the normal way from a larger research population. One way in which sampling can take place is through the process of one participant identifying another person known to them. In a study of people who engage in excessive consumption of alcohol, once the researcher has identified a first respondent, that person may be asked to nominate a second respondent. The second person could be asked whether or not they would be willing to participate, and this would enable them to consider their decision privately. Although this is clearly not a random sample, the system at least has the advantage that it generates respondents who are both willing to participate and also who are likely to be very well-informed respondents.

In general, much research in this area is concerned with the feelings of potential participants. The researcher is aware that the situation of many of the possible participants is far from ideal, and does not wish in any way to exacerbate those circumstances. It is often difficult to analyse the ethical issues involved in these areas of research, and sometimes the researcher may feel inclined to react rather spontaneously to a proposed research programme. For example, one researcher may propose to another that they embark on a project to interview people who have recently been made redundant. The second researcher may scarcely reflect upon the matter before saying 'That's an awful suggestion!' or 'You can't do that!' Such exclamations proclaim a spontaneous, emotional reaction to the suggestion, and exemplify what is known as emotive ethics or the emotive theory of ethics (see Box 6.8).

Box 6.8 Theoretical perspective: emotive ethics

Many theories of ethics derive from a careful analysis of the nature of the proposed moral action and of the potential consequences of the action. The emotive theory of ethics, on the other hand, points to an important feature of ethical utterances, and that is the spontaneous expression of a reaction towards something. If we see a child trying to stamp on woodlice in the garden, we may say something such as 'That's not nice! Stop that!' Not only would we be expressing a reaction but also, we would be indicating that the action should not be carried out. Although not the only form of ethical communication, emotive reactions of this sort are a common form of human ethical utterance (see Hudson 1970: 107).

The use of an emotive utterance can often convey ethical ideas in a succinct manner. For example, the first researcher who proposed the idea of interviewing people who had been made redundant is perhaps invited immediately to consider the feelings of people in this situation, and to reflect upon whether they would want to discuss the details of their circumstances so quickly after the event. An emotive approach to ethics is clearly not the only means for reacting to the ethics of this type of research, but it is an important form of communication.

7   The funding and sponsorship of research

Ethics and funding agreements

A significant amount of research, particularly large-scale projects, is supported by funding over and above that normally available to researchers. That is, the researchers do not finance the research from their own salaries or resources, but are the recipients of funding which is to be used specifically for that research project. The researchers often acquire such funding by submitting a competitive bid before the research commences. The funding agencies may be governments, charitable organizations, universities, research councils or bodies, or commercial organizations.

Fundamental to this chapter are the ethical issues raised by the support of research through dedicated research funding. Of course, all research is funded in some way. University lecturers who conduct small-scale research as part of their employment are funded through their salaries and therefore perhaps indirectly by the government. Part-time doctoral students may be funding their research through their own employment. This chapter is concerned with situations where a sponsor provides dedicated and often fairly substantial funding to support a particular research project. The question raised is whether and under what circumstances such an arrangement may alter the context or manner in which the research is conducted.

Let us start by trying to make out a case that there is nothing about the involvement of dedicated funding in research which has undesirable effects. The funding of research may have entirely desirable effects. It may enable the advancement of knowledge in circumstances where this would otherwise not be possible. It is only when the presence of additional funding alters the attitude of the sponsors and/or the researchers, to the manner in which the research would normally have been conducted, that the consequences may be undesirable.

It is possible, and perhaps understandable, that sponsors and researchers have different goals and aspirations in terms of a research programme. A commercial sponsor may have obligations, not least of which are to shareholders. The sponsor may need to see a return on the research investment, and hence will be primarily interested in outcomes which have commercial potential. This is not to say that commercial sponsors will be uninterested in the advancement of knowledge for its own sake. They may also realize that the advancement of understanding today may reveal commercial possibilities tomorrow. However, their primary interest is likely to be in commercial use of research outcomes. The researchers may be slightly less interested in commercial possibilities, and more concerned with making a contribution to knowledge. Such a dichotomy could be far too much of a generalization, and in many situations there may be a strong accord between the aims of the sponsor and those of the researcher.

What is important is that both sponsors and researchers cooperate in trying to ensure that the research is conducted in accord with accepted ethical standards. A useful general guide here is that the research should be carried out in broadly the same way as it would be conducted if it were not being funded by a sponsor. In other words, there is no general reason for the intervention of funding to alter the ethical standards of the research. The existence of funding may well change the general ownership of the products of the research, but that is a separate issue to the ethical standards applied during data collection.

It is important that there exists a carefully considered funding agreement or contract between the parties involved in the research. The two principal parties are likely to be the sponsor and the researcher, but there may also be other important parties such as the researcher's employment institution. The contract can have a positive role to play in the research arrangement because it can help to prevent later misunderstandings. It often causes the parties involved to think carefully about the proposed research and to try to anticipate problems and potential conflicts of interest. If these can be thoroughly discussed and as far as feasible resolved prior to the contract being agreed, then this should be to the advantage of everyone concerned.

There are many types of research which sponsors may be interested in supporting, such as certain types of pure research where there is a possibility of future commercial possibilities, although these may well be uncertain. Sponsors may be rather more interested in forms of research where attempts are being made to apply an existing discovery to the resolution of a practical problem. Some forms of social research may involve the collection and analysis of social data in order to explore the usefulness of a commercial product. Various forms of market research may be included within this category. There are then those forms of research which essentially involve the examination of the impact of commercial activities upon the environment or upon the community in general. Research of this type may involve a variety of activities. A group of people may be concerned that a company is having an adverse effect on the environment, in terms of erecting power lines, or electrical receivers, or chemical pollution. The company may commission a research organization to investigate such claims. In another case, people might be concerned about plans for a large-scale housing development, and the resultant effects upon the local community. The building company may commission some social research to investigate this. In other situations, a health authority may wish to restructure its hospital provision, or a local education authority may wish to merge and close some schools, and there may be complaints from some communities that they will be disadvantaged under the new arrangements. The organizations concerned may again identify researchers to analyse the claims.

All of these cases are distinguished by the common feature that the sponsors of the research will almost certainly hope for a specific outcome from the investigation. The electricity supply company will hope that the researchers find no ill effects from its power lines; the building company will hope that its housing plans are supported as likely to enhance the local community; and the local authority will hope that the researchers produce a positive evaluation of its plans for school restructuring. Not only will the sponsors in such cases have clear aspirations when they commission the research, but also their aspirations will be fully understood by the researchers who are successful in being selected to conduct the research. It is within the parameters of this situation that lie the possibility of differences of opinion over the conduct of the research. Such differences of opinion may involve ethical issues.

It is a fundamental requirement of research that the researcher should be able to conduct the research in an objective manner. In sponsored research, the sponsors clearly have an involvement in identifying the research questions. They are in effect paying to have certain issues investigated. However, once those questions have been identified and agreed, design of the research becomes the responsibility of the researchers. They should be free to develop a research design, plan a programme of data collection and analysis, and draw their conclusions without any reference to, or involvement with, the sponsors. Such independence of action and thought is fundamental to the research process.

It is important that when the results of the research are published, there should be a clear statement of the origin of the financial support for the research. This is significant in terms of maintaining the transparency of the research process. By placing such information in the public domain, the researchers are establishing their own independence. Other researchers or members of the public are free to read their conclusions. If they disagree with the research design, the manner in which the data were analysed, or the conclusions, they are free to engage in intellectual argument.

The declaration of financial support also enables the academic community and the broader public to see the research within the context of the sponsorship. The public can judge whether the key questions have been addressed in the research, and whether all significant factors have been taken into account. They can form their own judgement about whether they think the research has been influenced in any way by the sponsors. This is important both for the credibility of the research and also for the academic reputations of the researchers.

It could sometimes be the case that researchers hesitate to apply for sponsorship because of the nature of the commercial dealings of the proposed sponsor. Consider the ethical dilemma described in Box 7.1.

Box 7.1 Ethical dilemma: research sponsorship

A team of researchers is considering applying for a research contract with a multinational company. The research involves a study of the ways in which its staff relate to customers in its large retail outlets throughout Europe. The research team becomes aware, through reports in the media, of allegations that the company employs many thousands of staff in the developing world, often working in most unsatisfactory conditions. The company has defended itself by arguing that it adopts the best practices existing in a particular country at the time. It argues that it would be impracticable to try to adopt western European standards in a situation where these are not the norm. Some members of the research team feel that they should not apply for the contract, other members feel that they should seek assurances on some issues, while some are persuaded by the arguments of the company. Overall, the research team is unsure over the action to take.

There are many separate ethical issues here, and we have space to consider only some of the broad ethical problems. There may be some economic arguments in favour of not paying employees a standard wage in any country of the world, but one cannot feel that this morally justifies a company making excessive profits by paying its employees exceedingly low wages in a country which is very poor. However, there is a much stronger moral argument in terms of the conditions under which people work. While one might accept that people work for different wages in different countries, it is difficult to accept a situation in which human beings do not have the same protection in terms of health and safety. Here we are entering the realm of fundamental human rights, such as not being subject to unnecessary danger or suffering.

If we assume for the sake of argument that the company is not adopting the same health and safety standards in some developing countries, the researchers may feel that there is a strong case for not being involved in the research. If it can be shown that there are no valid reasons for not adopting the same health and safety standards, this further strengthens the moral case. The researchers may feel that in a world of global, integrated economies and communications that they cannot accept employees in one country being treated significantly less well than in another. They may further feel that if they applied for the contract, this would reflect adversely upon their own moral status. (The connection between sponsorship and research is discussed in Crow 2000: 78.)

The ethics of research contracts

A number of the principles mentioned are relevant to the content of research contracts. While it is reasonable for the sponsor to outline in the contract the research questions which they wish to have investigated, it is normally not acceptable for them to try to specify the data-collection methods which they would prefer the researchers to employ. The use of a large-scale survey may generate a large quantity of data, but those data may be fairly superficial. It may not adequately address the detail implicit in the research questions. On the other hand, the use of qualitative techniques may generate extremely detailed data, while the relatively small sample used may obscure any broad trends. Either of these techniques may or may not favour the sponsor's preferred outcome of the research, and for this reason it is preferable if the sponsor is not party to any decision about research methodology.

One of the most important products of any research project is the research report. The researcher should have the freedom to write such a report, without having a contractual obligation to have it approved by the sponsor. This principle is founded in the broad distinction between the rights of the researcher in terms of the research data and analysis, and the rights of the sponsor in terms of the commercial potential of the research. For the researcher, the main ethical principle involved is that of academic and intellectual freedom. This does not mean that researchers are free to investigate issues in any way that they choose, nor to draw whatever conclusions they wish, however illogical. There are many constraints upon their work. If they are employed by an academic institution, they are expected to conduct themselves in a professional manner, and there are many reviews and checks of their work. Fellow researchers in the research team are able to check each other's results and analysis. Once the outcomes of a research project are published, other specialists in the field can attempt to replicate the investigation and results. One important aspect of such checks and balances is that the research is assessed by people of comparable expertise. The sponsor may or may not have such expertise. Nevertheless, the crucial issue is that those assessing the work do so from a point of view of objectivity and disinterest. They have no interest in the outcomes of the research supporting a particular viewpoint. The sponsors, on the other hand, may prefer that the data analysis suggests a particular result. It is important that any changes to these broad principles should be thoroughly discussed and agreed before entering them in the research contract.

The resolution of potential conflicts of interest

If a contract has been carefully prepared and worded, and if its preparation was preceded by balanced discussion of the interests of the relevant parties, it should help to minimize the possibility of any conflicts either during or after the research. It should specify the obligations and responsibilities which the different parties owe to each other. Nevertheless, conflicts of interest may still occur.

In a situation involving the sponsorship of research, the most likely source of conflict is that between the academic demands of the research project, and the demands from the sponsor's viewpoint to capitalize upon the commercial development of the product. Consider the ethical dilemma described in Box 7.2.

Box 7.2   Ethical dilemma: conflict between academic and commercial interests

A small team of researchers is conducting a study of the housing needs of elderly residents, and in particular of the internal fixtures and fittings needed. Although the researchers had originally intended to employ a questionnaire and a small number of interviews to collect data from the sample, they formed the view during the research, that they ought to carry out more interviews to enrich the data. The sponsors, who were a specialist housing development company, disagreed with the change, because it was likely to slow down the production of the final report by about two months. In commercial terms, this was a considerable amount of time. The contract did give the researchers the freedom to amend the data-collection process in the light of the developing nature of the research. On the other hand, the contract did specify a delivery date for the research report. The date would hence be exceeded by about two months if the researchers made their changes to the number of interviews to be carried out.

In any contractual situation, there may well be legal issues involved. However, in order to help us explore the ethical issues involved in this case, it may be better to assume for the sake of argument that both parties wish to avoid litigation. To look at the situation from the sponsor's point of view, a two-month delay is a long period. The building company may have a complex schedule of work contracts pending, among which this is simply one job. They commissioned the researchers to tell them of the housing needs of elderly people and need this information on time, if there is not going to be the necessity to try to change a complex schedule. They feel that there was a clear agreement in the contract to submit the research report by a particular time, and that the researchers are morally and legally obliged to do that.

The researchers have been disappointed with the results from the questionnaire and the early interviews. They feel that their data have been unusually limited, and although they understand the point of view of the sponsors, they are concerned that the data they obtain should be sufficiently valid to provide a sound basis for the building design. They are aware that they should provide the report by a certain time, but also wish to exercise what they see as their right to amend the data-collection process where necessary.

One might argue in cases such as these that if the research data are flawed, the commercial decisions which are founded upon them will also be flawed. Hence it could be suggested that if the quality of the commercial decisions depends upon the quality of the research, an initial emphasis should be placed upon the latter. Nevertheless, a general sense of fairness suggests that it would be unreasonable for the researchers to suggest changing the submission date for the report by a great deal. There is every indication that this is a situation where a compromise is required.

Situations such as these, involving researcher and sponsor, are often practical situations, which could be said to require the application of a good deal of common sense. In such circumstances it may be less easy to apply theoretical criteria, or broad principles to resolve any ethical issues. It can often be a case of considering the practical context of a specific set of circumstances. One philosophical approach to this type of problem is that of pragmatism (see Box 7.3).

Box 7.3   Theoretical perspective: pragmatism and ethics

Pragmatism is a school of philosophy which is based very much on the work of William James and John Dewey. The essence of pragmatism is that purely theoretical analysis of philosophical problems is insufficient, and that it should be complemented by a very practical approach to issues. Many approaches to ethical problems attempt to develop general principles which are then applied to a specific issue. A pragmatic approach to ethics tends to take the view that such an approach is rather mistaken. A pragmatist would tend to take the view that although it is sensible to try to develop general ethical principles, one should not assume that these will be relevant to all situations, nor should they be viewed as being rigid and unalterable. In fact, moral principles should be seen as developing and changing, depending upon our experience of practical ethical situations (see Loewy 1996: 28).

Pragmatists would support their practical approach to ethical issues by arguing that the social world is always in a state of flux. As the world changes, completely new types of moral problems are created. We have only to think of the impact of advances in human genetics, for example, to realize the variety of ethical issues that are now arising. In addition, the broad consensus in society, in relation to different issues, does not remain the same. Views on ethical issues do change, and this applies as much to research ethics as to any other area. Hence, pragmatists would probably argue that moral principles should be to some extent flexible, and should derive to some considerable extent from a consideration of the practical moral issues with which we have to contend.

The issue of allowing sponsors to read or edit draft research reports

Before we discuss some of the issues within this subject, we should try to clarify one or two points about the ownership of the report, since some questions would appear to follow from this. First, a research report is a product of the academic and intellectual activity of a group of researchers. It represents the manner in which they have analysed a problem, and then set out to collect data to investigate it. The report encapsulates all of this; in addition, it states their findings and conclusions. It does not represent the intellectual activity of the sponsors. They may have enabled the research to take place, but the final report is the work of the researchers and not of the sponsors.

Second, it is often normal with a research report, as with other types of writing, to produce a first draft. This may be read by the author or authors, and amended where necessary for anything from typographical errors to errors of fact or analysis. The authors or researchers may wish to pass the report on to someone outside the team for checking, but this would normally be an academic peer or colleague. It may be far less appropriate to pass the draft to the sponsor for comment, as this could be construed as an invitation to amend it.

There are two principal reasons for it not being desirable for sponsors to amend a research report. First, they may not have the academic and research expertise to make informed judgements about such issues as methodology. Second, and importantly, there may be the temptation to ask for changes to either the wording or the nature of the conclusions, if these were seen as being contrary to the interests of the sponsors. In the case of some research projects, the sponsors may not be concerned about the actual findings of the report, as long as they receive specific advice on appropriate action. In other cases, however, the sponsors may hope that the researchers draw conclusions which are beneficial in some way to the sponsors. Even with the most scrupulous of sponsors, it may be difficult for them to distinguish situations where they are requesting changes because they feel the report is inaccurate in some way, and where they want changes because the report's findings are inconvenient to them. The danger of these two issues becoming merged or fused is one of the main reasons why it is preferable if sponsors are not able to make changes to the research report. Even the possibility that changes might be countenanced could arguably undermine the status of the research and the report. One of the most important indicators of the quality, validity and value of a research report is the assurance of academic independence. In order to secure this independence, it is preferable if all draft versions of the report are retained with the research team or its advisers, and released into the public domain only when it is in a finished form.

There is one possible justification for allowing sponsors to read the report, after it has been finalized, yet before it is released into the public domain. This justification is that the sponsors may wish to produce a short public statement commenting upon the research, and raising any issues or concerns which they feel may not have been adequately addressed. In most cases the sponsors may not wish to do this. However, particularly in situations where the sponsors may not agree with some aspects of the report, and where they feel that some relevant circumstances have not been taken into account, it may be reasonable to give them the opportunity to produce a statement in advance of publication. The research report and the sponsor's statement would then move into the public domain at the same time, and others could form their own judgements. It should be added that exceptionally there may be some specific contractual situations where the sponsor may own the research report and the rights to dissemination. These may be unusual circumstances, and many researchers may feel that they would not wish to be involved in such a contract. Nevertheless, such situations are possible.

Normally one of the ethical principles inherent in research situations is that of being open about access to information and arguments. It is the principle of acknowledging that there are different views on the same issue, and of creating an environment in which those divergent viewpoints can find a voice. It is the principle of being transparent about the manner in which those views are made public, and of not trying to obscure viewpoints which may be either inconvenient to oneself, or contrary to one's own position. It is important that researchers adhere to such principles, because, among other reasons, a spirit of openness helps to assure a reputation for honesty and credibility for researchers. The argument of abiding by ethical principles because they result in a desirable end, is a form of consequentialist argument. There are other justifications for such principles, and what are sometimes termed deontological arguments are examples of these (see Box 7.4).

Within this broad ethical perspective one might argue then that openness

---

Box 7.4   Theoretical perspective: deontological arguments

Some ethical theories can be described as consequentialist, because they seek to justify actions by pointing to the supposed desirable outcomes which those actions are likely to produce. On such an explanation, people tell the truth, for example, because it makes them feel better, or because perhaps the world is an easier place in which to live when we can all rely upon the truth of what people say. Deontological arguments look much more at the nature of the moral decisions themselves, than upon the assumed consequences. On such a view, truth telling is morally desirable simply because we all have a general ethical responsibility to tell the truth. Deontology is associated with, among others, the work of Immanuel Kant and W.D. Ross (see Husted and Husted 1995: 10).

---

with regard to information is simply a good thing, partly at least because we have a responsibility to behave with such transparency towards our fellow human beings. Whichever form of argument one prefers, it seems desirable that certain pieces of information are included in a research report. It has generally become the practice to include in academic journal articles and in research reports the names of research sponsors. This is not only as a courtesy to thank them for their financial support, but also as an implicit reassurance to readers that sponsorship has not affected the conduct of the research, nor the manner in which conclusions were drawn. In terms of transparency, it is also important that any specific parameters to the research which were negotiated between the researchers and the sponsors from the inception of the project are described in the report. This again helps to remove any doubts that the researchers may have been influenced by the demands of sponsors.

Intellectual ownership

Research is often a team effort, and many individuals contribute to the design and conduct of the research. A relatively small group of people may develop the bid for research sponsorship, while being supported by a larger group of people who it is anticipated will contribute by collecting data, or performing some routine data analysis. Once the research has been completed, it may be disseminated and published in a variety of ways. Research students who have been involved may write up a selected part of the research for a doctoral study. Some of the findings may be written up by the lead researchers as an academic journal article or a series of articles. In some cases a book may result. There will certainly be a formal research report, and perhaps an executive summary of that report. Conference papers are another source of dissemination. Whichever range of methods is actually employed, one issue which is certain to arise is that of authorship, and in particular, that of multiple authorship.

There are a number of separate ethical issues to be considered here. First, a selection has sometimes to be made about the individuals who will be listed as authors at the beginning of a book or journal article. Second, as a connected issue, the names of some people are included at the end of the article or book as having made a contribution, but not at the level to justify being signified as an author. Finally, there is the not inconsiderable matter of determining the order of the names of multiple authors.

It is important to decide on criteria for determining those who should be considered the main authors of a research report or article. It seems reasonable that the principal criterion should be to consider the intellectual contribution made by individuals to the report. This would appear to be rather more fair than taking into account the academic status of an individual. According to this view, a person should not normally be listed as a principal author or contributor merely because they occupy a senior academic post in a university. The prime consideration should be the actual academic contribution which has been made.

It is not always straightforward to form a judgement about the principal authors. For example, a university professor may have had the initial idea for a piece of research, and may have made an initial approach to a funding body. A small group of lecturers may have done most of the work in preparing the funding proposal, even though the professor's name was included. During the actual research, a considerable amount of the actual data collection may have been conducted by a group of research assistants. The data analysis and the writing of the first draft of the research report may have been carried out by the lecturers. The professor and one of the lecturers may then have carried out a careful editing of the report. This is simply by way of an example, and in reality the way in which the different tasks might be apportioned could be even more complicated. As a broad principle, those who have made a significant contribution to the research and to the report should be listed as authors of the report. If research assistants have been carrying out fairly routine data collection, and this has been under the specific direction of, say, a lecturer, it may be considered that this is insufficient to merit the status of author. The contribution of the research assistants should be noted at the end of the report.

The order in which the authors are named may be of considerable importance. It may be perceived by some as an indicator of the importance of the contribution to the research, with the first-named author being the most significant. The name of the first-named author may also be used far more when the research report or article is cited in other publications or is indexed. It is helpful, and avoids misunderstandings, if the authors agree among themselves the system of ordering which they will use. They may prefer a simple system of alphabetical ordering by surname. However, arguably from an ethical viewpoint, an attempt should be made to agree upon an order which reflects the intellectual contribution to the research. This order should take into account the design and conduct of the research, as well as the writing of the report. In other words, there should be an assessment of the overall contribution made. The final ordering should not, in this view, consider the relative academic status in an institution.

Sometimes a single major research study may generate a series of journal articles, which may be published in different journals for some considerable time after the original research was conducted. When this is the case, it may be necessary to reconsider the way in which authorship is attributed. For example, a research student who was helping with the research and collected some of the data may have an agreement that some data may be used towards a doctorate. That student may wish to write up an article based on a subset of the data. It seems reasonable that the research student's name should be listed first. The research student may feel that there is a case to include also the names of one or two lecturers who may have provided significant help with the article. Such names should normally be included only if the contribution has been significant, and the names should be listed after that of the research student.

The fundamental ethical issue in such situations is about fairness to those who have made a contribution to the research. As we have seen there are many possible permutations of the ways in which different people may contribute to a research programme. Individual circumstances have to be taken into account. (Issues of intellectual ownership are discussed in Townend 2000: 92–6.)

In conclusion, much research, particularly large-scale research, will always require some financial backing; commercial undertakings will often need to be underpinned by research. There remains no intrinsic reason why this should not be a truly symbiotic relationship, with both interests gaining from the other. Nevertheless, there remains the potential for judgements to be swayed, and hence the relevance of ethical considerations in research sponsorship.

8 The publication and dissemination of research

Different audiences for research reports and findings

Researchers normally try to publish a report of their research. Such dissemination is advantageous in a variety of ways. First, it enables other researchers to familiarize themselves with the research and analysis. As a result of this they may wish either to try to replicate the research, or to extend it by doing comparable research in a different context. Second, the report may encourage other researchers in the same broad field to look at their data in a slightly different way, and hence to gain fresh insights.

Third, the reporting of research puts academics and researchers into contact with each other. Research often progresses more effectively when people can collaborate and share ideas with each other. Researchers might arrange to meet at conferences, to write joint academic papers or books, or to develop new research proposals. Fourth, research reporting enables potential research students to know the names of those academics who are carrying out work in areas in which they are interested. Hence research students may be able to apply to appropriate university departments in order to register for a research degree. Finally, underlying all of these interwoven advantages of dissemination is the undeniable result of promoting the academic reputations and careers of individual researchers. Although this may not be the prime motive, it may be an associated result. Researchers are often quite rightly proud of the work they have accomplished, and understandably hope to achieve some peer recognition for this.

There are a variety of ways in which research may be disseminated and published. Arguably the main genre for research publishing is the academic journal article. There are many academic journals published by a wide range of publishing organizations. Some journals publish articles only within a rather narrow academic specialism, while others draw on material from a much broader subject area. Most journals aspire to an international readership and to receiving articles from research institutions around the world. Journals also usually try to have an editorial board which includes leading academics from universities in different countries. Most serious academic journals adopt a system of peer review, whereby an article is submitted to at least two academic referees for comment before being accepted. The broad agreement of the referees is usually required before the article is accepted for publication. Journals which adopt a system such as this often describe themselves as a 'fully refereed' journal.

The academic journal article is a particular genre of writing and has certain well-defined characteristics. Although different journals have their own specific requirements in terms of style of presentation of article and length, a typical journal article might be of about 6000–8000 words in length. This length requirement imposes some restrictions on researchers, and usually has an impact in terms of the amount of primary data which can be included. A journal article may be used to report a small-scale piece of research, in which case the article almost represents the equivalent of a research report. The article may include a significant quantity of the original data collected. In other circumstances, the article may represent only a small section of a much larger research project. In this case the author has to be careful in terms of selecting material which will adhere to the word limit. It is important that care is taken to include at least a mention of all the critical aspects of the research. For example, the researcher may simply mention the number of respondents who provided data, without explaining the basis upon which they were chosen. If the abbreviation of the research design is excessive, it may result in an article which raises a good many questions in the mind of the reader. There is an ethical issue inasmuch as the author is almost asking for the reader to accept the methodology as an act of faith. Normally, such limitations would be identified and corrected as a result of the peer review process. Nevertheless, the length of the typical journal article does create restrictions for the author.

Academic journals have a fairly specialized audience, consisting of academics and students who are interested in or researching the subject. The style of a journal article is usually formal, and hence will probably appeal only to an academic audience. If researchers wish to disseminate their work to a wider audience, it may be more appropriate to select a professional journal. Such journals are intended for a readership within a particular vocational area. For example, journals may be devoted to practical issues for social workers or primary school teachers. Some articles may still report the outcomes of research, but they do not devote much space to issues of methodology or analysis. There will be a tendency to concentrate upon the key findings and to discuss the implications of these for professional practice. Articles for professional journals will normally be subject to editorial control, but perhaps not to an extensive academic refereeing process.

One of the inevitable difficulties with research dissemination is the time taken from the completion of the research until an article appears in a journal.

If a researcher starts to prepare an article for an academic journal as soon as a research project has ended, it may take several months to write the article. By the time the refereeing process has been completed, and the article allocated to a specific journal issue for production, an additional 12 months may have expired. The process from the initial concept of the article to it finally appearing in print may take 15 months. The process for a professional journal will probably be much quicker: the articles are typically much shorter, and the refereeing process, if it occurs, is not usually as detailed. The time taken for publication may be an issue for researchers if they wish to publicize their research quickly.

Other means of disseminating research include writing chapters in edited books, or writing an authored book. Having the opportunity to write a chapter in a book to be edited by another person would usually depend upon the researcher knowing someone who was planning to edit a book on a relevant subject. The proposed chapter would need to be appropriate to the general topic and approach of the book. An authored book would clearly be a much larger undertaking and require considerable planning. If we consider the time from the development of the original concept until publication, both edited books and authored books would take considerably longer to produce than an academic journal article. In terms of sheer speed of dissemination, one of the best forms of publication may be newspapers. Some daily newspapers have specialist weekly sections devoted to education or the social sciences, and publish accounts of recent research. Such accounts may have a greater likelihood of publication if the research is relevant to contemporary issues and is of interest to the readership. In some areas such as education, there are weekly newspapers devoted to the subject, which also provide an outlet for articles summarizing recent research findings. (A wide range of aspects of academic writing is discussed in Richardson 1994: 516–29.)

It is important that when research is described in such contexts, the more populist style of writing does not amend the nature the research and the findings. It is not always easy to rewrite something from an academic style into a popular style, and still to retain with fidelity the academic content of the original.

Another genre of writing for the dissemination of research is the paper delivered at an academic conference. Depending upon the manner in which they are to be delivered, papers can vary in length quite considerably. They will generally be subjected to a process of academic review, which may be repeated in a different form if the papers are to be collected together and published after the conference. The audience for the paper will be largely academic. One significant advantage of the conference paper for reporting research is that the waiting time between completion of the research and dissemination may be fairly short.

One final issue about reporting research is that it is important to try to fulfil the obligations of the researchers in terms of presenting practical recommendations to a research sponsor. In many cases of sponsorship, the funding organization will hope for specific advice to emerge from the study. If this is the case, the researchers should not normally expect the sponsor to carry out interpretative work on the research results. They should normally try to interpret the results in terms of implications for the sponsor, which need not necessarily involve a recommendation of specific action. Rather it may involve explaining a number of options along with the advantages and disadvantages of each, in order to help the sponsor decide upon a course of action. (For a discussion of the reporting of research, see Gilbert 1993: 328–44.)

Editorial procedures in academic journals

As we have discussed, there are a number of different vehicles for the publication of research; the most common is the academic journal. It is important that the procedures employed by journals are ethical in approach, and among other features, ensure that each article submitted is treated in a similar way and judged fairly. The number and quality of articles published in academic journals also play a significant part in establishing the reputations of researchers and academics; it is important therefore that the systems used by journals are valid and consistent. University departments are judged at least partly on the quality of their research output; one of the measures of such quality is the nature of the articles published by the departmental staff in journals. One outcome of a good research assessment may be enhanced funding for that department. It can thus be seen that journals are of no small significance in the academic world.

Before examining the different ethical issues which can arise in terms of publishing in academic journals, let us consider the main features of the modus operandi of journals. There are two broad aspects to the functioning of journals. The publishing, financial, marketing and distribution aspects of the journal are typically dealt with by the publishers, while the academic decisions concerning the selection and revision of the articles is dealt with by a group of editors who are typically employed as lecturers and academics, but are also involved with the journal as part of their normal academic activities. There is often a single editor who takes practical day-to-day decisions, along with a fairly large group of academics who constitute an editorial board. One of the main functions of the members of the editorial board is to review the articles which are submitted to the journal. A journal may have an assistant editor, and also a book reviews editor, who organizes the reviewing of books submitted to the journal by publishers. It is fairly common for people to submit reviews of books they have read to a journal; the book reviews editor collates such submissions and edits them where necessary. In most journals there is considerable interaction between the academic functions of the journal and the publishers. We can think of these functions as constituting two broad divisions of responsibility. There is clearly considerable variation in the constitution of individual journals, but we have given an outline of a fairly typical structure.

The ethical issues inherent in the process of publishing an article tend to occur at the point where decisions are taken, and when those decisions are conveyed to authors. Given the place of journal article publishing, at the heart of the research process, it is important that sufficient consideration is given to these processes and procedures.

The first key decision is when the editor sends the article to the reviewers. The latter should be chosen on the basis of their understanding and expertise of both the subject matter of the article and of the methodology used. It is important that a journal has an editorial board composed of a group of people representing a wide range of research traditions and perspectives, and also with an understanding of the full range of subject matter on which the journal is likely to receive contributions. This is likely to be achieved only if the journal adopts a carefully considered policy on the appointment of new members of its editorial board. The board should include academics and researchers from institutions in a variety of countries and cultures. The board should be as balanced as possible in terms of gender and ethnicity. They should all be familiar with the broad subject matter of the journal, but should also as individuals have specialisms which collectively enable them to comment on the range of articles received. The central ethical issue here is one of fairness to authors. Their articles should be considered in an objective manner by well-informed reviewers.

On the assumption that the editorial board represents a sufficiently broad range of expertise, it is important that the editor is able to allocate an article to the most appropriately qualified reviewers. This clearly necessitates the editor being able to judge the article in terms of content and methodology. Authors would not wish their articles to be reviewed by academics who were non-specialists in the area of their article, and if editors are not confident of allocating the article to a particular specialism, then advice should be sought.

The next stage of decision-making involves the reviewers deciding on the merits of the article, and whether it is suitable for publication. It is important here that journals have developed clear criteria by which articles are to be judged. Some of these criteria may derive from the notes for contributors published in the journal. For example, the article may need to be a certain length, to include an abstract, and to use a certain form of referencing and citation system. There may be a number of other criteria, however, including such aspects as style of academic writing, the manner in which arguments are presented, the explanation of the methodology and the way in which conclusions are drawn. It is essential that reviewers apply these criteria in a consistent manner, and that each article is treated in as similar a manner as possible. The existence of a set of criteria enhances the ethics of the process, in that it helps to ensure that all articles are treated in as fair a way as possible.

The reviewers normally annotate the manuscript indicating what they regard as deficiencies of content or argument. Unless they accept an article without the need for any further revision, the reviewers should produce a report which clearly indicates the revisions necessary to make the article suitable for publication. If the report is sufficiently precise, the key issues can easily be conveyed by the editor to the author, and the editor can subsequently check that these amendments have been made. The spirit of this process is that the editor relies very much upon the specialist academic judgement of the reviewers. The latter thus have an important role to play. Within the sphere of academic journal publishing, they are in effect the guardians of the quality of the way in which research is published. Their decisions also have the wider implications which we have mentioned earlier.

Reviewers thus have great responsibilities to the authors, to the editor and editorial board of the journal, to the publishers, and to the wider academic community. If they do not do their job consistently and rigorously, this may result in a decline in the reputation of a journal, with implications for a variety of people, including the publishers. For the reviewing process to be at all meaningful, it should involve, as far as possible, the dispassionate application of criteria. Reviewers should not favour one article rather than another, simply because it is the kind of article which they would personally prefer to see in the journal. Questions of personal taste should be irrelevant. Decisions should be made on the basis of the agreed procedures and criteria for the journal. If the reviewers feel that an article is completely unsuitable for the journal, and that it cannot realistically be revised, they should try to indicate in as clear, yet sensitive, a manner as possible, the reasons for the article not meeting the standards of the journal. The editor will need to use these reasons to construct an appropriate letter of rejection to the author.

Once an editor has received comments from the two reviewers, then they have to make the final decision about acceptance or rejection. This is straightforward if the reviewers are in agreement. In that case, the article can be rejected, accepted subject to specified amendments, or accepted unconditionally. If the reviewers differ in their conclusions, the editor's role becomes more complex. Consider the dilemma described in Box 8.1.

Perhaps the first point to make here is that the dearth of articles for the next issue should not affect the decision about the current article. If there are insufficient articles being submitted to the journal, this is a separate issue which could be addressed by a marketing policy or by inviting submissions on specific topics. From an ethical point of view, the editor would seem to have a clear responsibility, and that is to apply the journal's publishing criteria in as balanced a manner as possible.

Box 8.1 Ethical dilemma: editorial judgement

A journal editor receives reports on an article from two reviewers. The first reviewer recommends that the article should be rejected outright, because the subject matter of the article is only peripherally connected with the main subject matter of the journal, and also that the writing style is far too colloquial for an academic journal. The reviewer feels that the author has such an insufficient grasp of an academic writing style that a revision would not be feasible. The second reviewer agrees with the two main criticisms of the first reviewer. However, the second reviewer feels that the writing style can be corrected if appropriate advice is given, and indeed provides detailed annotations on the manuscript. The second reviewer also points out that the journal has published several articles in the past, which were only tangentially connected with the core subject of the journal. The second reviewer recommends acceptance subject to appropriate amendments to the writing style. The editor is unsure on the action to take, and sends the article to a third reviewer. This reviewer again criticizes the style, and recommends acceptance subject to the article being rewritten. However, this reviewer argues that it is not the job of the reviewers to provide advice on English grammar and style, and does not include any suggested amendments, but argues that the rewriting should be left to the author. The reviewer also feels that the subject can be considered broadly within the scope of the journal.

The editor is currently under some pressure from the publishers to provide more articles. The forthcoming issue urgently requires two more articles if it is to have its normal number of pages. The editor is reflecting on the appropriate action to take with regard to the article.

If we assume that it is one of the criteria of the journal that articles should be written in an appropriate academic style, it may well be that all three reviewers actually tried to comply with the criterion. All three reviewers may have formed exactly the same opinion about the standard of the writing. They simply differed in terms of whether it was realistic to expect the author to revise it. The first reviewer presumably felt that there was insufficient evidence to encourage the view that the author would be able to revise the article; the second reviewer felt that it was feasible with assistance; and the third reviewer believed it was possible, but that the journal should not provide any help.

Eventually, the editor tried to identify a course of action which represented something of a compromise between the views of all three reviewers. She wrote to the author indicating that the journal would in principle be willing to publish a revised version, but that only one attempt at revision would be accepted. If that was not satisfactory, then the article would be rejected. She also attempted to distinguish between several errors where there was an element of perhaps academic misunderstanding. Here she gave fairly detailed direction in terms of potential revision. In the majority of cases, where the errors were primarily of a grammatical or stylistic nature, she adopted a different policy. She identified single examples of a number of generic errors which had been repeated several times in the article, and explained why the writing was unsatisfactory. The identification and correction of the recurring errors was then left to the author. The editor also took the view that the editorial policy in the past had not involved a particularly restrictive approach to the subject matter of articles, hence that there was no justification to reject the article on the grounds of academic subject.

Once the editor has made the decision about the way to treat an article, the final stage in the process is to convey this to the author. In the case of articles requiring revisions the editor may send to the author the actual comments from the reviewers, with their names removed to preserve anonymity. In other cases, an editor may produce a synopsis of the comments from the reviewers. Ethical issues are perhaps most predominant at this stage in the case of articles which are to be rejected. The editor has to decide whether to simply reject the article and to wish the author good fortune in placing it elsewhere, or to offer some advice in terms of preparing it for publication in another journal.

If one takes the view that editors have a moral responsibility beyond their own journals to the wider academic community, it seems only reasonable to provide some advice to the rejected author. Whatever the perceived quality of an article, the author will still have spent a considerable amount of time in researching and writing it, and will inevitably be disappointed at the rejection. Perhaps an editor should first try to explain clearly the reasons for rejection, while at the same time expressing these in language which is not too discouraging. The author could then be advised on what were considered to be the strengths of the article, and on how these could be used as the basis of a restructured article. Finally, the editor might remind the author of the importance of reading published articles in the journal to which it is proposed to submit, in order to try to emulate the format and style. A kindly, supportive and advisory letter from an editor may give fresh impetus to a new author who might otherwise lose motivation. The journal editor's role is increasingly significant in an academic world which appears to be focused more and more on the importance of publications.

The nature of plagiarism

Plagiarism is the use of another person's ideas or writing without any acknowledgement of the source of that material. There are many different aspects to plagiarism, however, and some of these raise ethical issues that are far from clear. Plagiarism is not easy to clarify; it is a far from easy task to determine the conceptual boundaries of the term. The only way to determine those boundaries is to discuss a variety of incidents which we suspect may constitute plagiarism, and to try to resolve whether they constitute an example of our concept.

Perhaps we may begin by examining some examples of behaviour which at least appear to be within the concept of plagiarism. If an author was writing a research report and included a substantial section of several paragraphs which had been copied from another publication, and did not indicate either the source or even that it had been obtained from another source, we might reasonably class this as plagiarism. It may occur to us that there may be mitigating circumstances in any case of plagiarism, if it could be shown that the writer had no intent to plagiarize but simply made an error of some kind. However, in this case it seems rather unlikely that a writer could include several paragraphs without any intent whatsoever. This is perhaps so if we are discussing exclusively hand-written material, but in a computer age, a writer or researcher may make a different defence. The writer may claim that although the research report certainly does contain some material from another source, there was no specific intent to plagiarize; indeed the material could have been introduced only through inadvertent transfer from another electronic file.

Here are the beginnings of some ethical complications. We can begin to distinguish between an act of plagiarism, and the intent to bring about that act. Plagiarism could conceivably be carried out with intent or without intent. We may need to reflect upon whether a person stands condemned by an act of plagiarism alone, or whether it is the proven intent to plagiarize which is the key offence.

A second example of plagiarism is a situation where a research report or article contains a very small section which has been apparently copied from another source, without acknowledging that source. Let us suppose, for the sake of argument, that the section involved is only one sentence. Some people may wish to question whether this should be included within a definition of plagiarism at all. Some may say that while it may technically be plagiarism, common sense suggests that there is a lower limit to the length of the copied extract beyond which the copying is so minimal that for all practical purposes it should not be regarded as plagiarism. This appears to be a fairly plausible argument, although perhaps we should press it further by reflecting on whether, to take an extreme case, the unauthorized copying of a single word could constitute plagiarism. Clearly, the copying of words such as 'and' or the definite article would not be regarded as plagiarism. However, suppose we consider the use of a single technical term which has been developed by a leading academic for use in specific circumstances. If that term is now used by others without acknowledging the original source, that may well constitute plagiarism. This is not to say that every technical and specialist term must be acknowledged. There arguably comes a point when a particular idea or concept has become so well disseminated and understood that there would no longer appear to be a need to cite the original source. For example, in a discussion of positivistic approaches to social science research, we may not feel the necessity to mention our indebtedness to Auguste Comte. We may discuss his contribution to social science and indeed wish to evaluate his application of the methods of the natural sciences to those of the social sciences, but we may perhaps feel no necessary obligation to do so. To sum up, there would appear to be no minimum limit to the length of an extract which might be involved in an act of plagiarism; in addition, there is the potentially complex issue of whether the spirit of intent is necessary before someone may be accused of plagiarism.

Quite apart from any notion of intent, there is an important question about the nature of the content of plagiarized material. There is probably little dispute about a situation where one author copies a passage from another author. There is a rather more complex question about the use of ideas and arguments taken from one author and expressed in the words of a second author. There may be a situation where an idea or concept is closely associated with the work of a particular writer or researcher. In such cases, the unauthorized and uncited use of an idea might be construed as plagiarism. For this type of situation to be defined as plagiarism, it would arguably have to be demonstrated that the idea or concept was still specifically associated with the original author, and had not in any sense passed into common use. Admittedly each situation would have to be considered on its merits, but there would appear to be a point at which ideas do, in a sense, become the shared property of the academic community. It may often be the case that an idea will pass into common use, and yet still be remembered as having been developed by a specific writer or academic. There is then probably a certain degree of freedom over whether it is absolutely necessary to quote the originator of the idea. Sometimes it may seem relevant to do so, and at others it may seem perfectly reasonable to omit a specific reference to the originator. To omit the reference would possibly not open the writer to accusations of plagiarism.

A further dimension is that it is often difficult to define precisely the origin of many ideas in education and the social sciences. It is not always easy to trace back an idea or an argument to one particular research paper. It may be that several researchers were working simultaneously on a particular idea, and it is difficult to credit one individual with that idea. Even though a particular social science concept may have had a single origin in time, many different writers and academics may have added ideas to the original concept. The concept assumes an evolving nature rather than retaining its original use; in such cases the term acquires a form of common ownership. So many writers have added a further dimension to the concept that it ceases to be regarded as the preserve of an individual. For these kinds of reasons, it may be difficult to decide whether plagiarism has taken place.

Quite apart from the written content of research reports and articles, there is the question of plagiarizing data. This could occur where a researcher takes data collected by another researcher, and uses it for reanalysis, perhaps for a totally different piece of research. Assuming that the researcher taking the data did not ask permission for the new use, this might be construed as plagiarism. On one level, it might be regarded as poor research, since the researcher carrying out the reanalysis would not necessarily be familiar with the circumstances under which the data had been collected, which might be very significant for the new research. Certainly, the use of the data without permission would be ethically questionable.

It may be considered that where one researcher uses a research design or a novel means of analysing data, that it could constitute plagiarism if it has been employed by someone else. However, it is often difficult to demonstrate that the other researcher did not acquire at least part of the idea for the research from someone else, and so on. So rapidly do ideas circulate in the contemporary world that it is often difficult to trace ideas back to their supposed originators. These difficulties are exacerbated in a world of mass communications and the Internet. New ideas circulate very easily.

Sometimes the expression of text by one author in different words written by another is considered to be plagiarism. Such paraphrasing needs to be analysed further. If researcher A rewrites, in completely different language, a passage written by researcher B that cannot be plagiarism, which is defined in terms of the unauthorized replication of a written passage. The original passage is not being replicated. The logic of the situation seems to suggest that it may be plagiarism only on the grounds of the unauthorized and uncited replication of ideas. Hence we return to the problems already mentioned about the potential plagiarism of ideas.

There are circumstances where the paraphrasing of text may appear to involve plagiarism. Consider, for example, the case of one researcher paraphrasing a section from a research report which describes the results of the analysis of the data. It would seem to be a reasonable assumption that the results of an analysis of data are seen as belonging to the researcher who carried out the analysis. In other words, the ideas inherent in that analysis and the results are closely associated with the researcher who conducted the analysis. Therefore to paraphrase such a passage, without any acknowledgement or citation, could be construed as involving plagiarism. A related way in which plagiarism might be felt to have taken place involves a researcher using data collected by research assistants, but without acknowledging their assistance. Whether or not such an event might be accurately felt to involve plagiarism may depend on a variety of factors, but it would seem to be at least a courtesy to mention the names of those who have assisted in the collection of data.

To return briefly to the question of intent, an act of plagiarism has occurred if a passage has been copied into a new document, but there may be doubt as to whether the person who did this is morally culpable. When people are transferring material from one electronic file to another with great rapidity, it may be understandable if sometimes material is inadvertently included. Ideally such mistakes should not happen, but we should concede their possibility, and equally the potential for unintentional plagiarism.

The style of expression of academic judgements

It is important that the conclusions of a programme of research are expressed in a way which follows clearly and logically from the data. In one sense, this is an issue within the scope of the philosophy of knowledge, and concerns the criteria which we adopt in order to try to determine whether or not we believe something to be true. Such epistemological concerns are central to the determination of truth and falsity. However, it is arguable that interwoven with these questions are matters of ethics. The latter are concerned with such matters as the manner in which we convey research results to others, and the motives which we hold in so doing. Researchers, whether they like it or not, almost inevitably occupy an influential role. People listen to their opinions, and often change their behaviour patterns as a result of what they are told by researchers. This places a special responsibility upon academics and researchers, not only to conduct research according to certain well-established procedures, but also to disseminate it in a manner which follows logically from the data, and does not exaggerate any element of the research.

Researchers should not express their results in such a manner that they exceed the reasonable limitations of the data, or else unreasonably emphasize one section of the data compared with another. To do this would not be good science, and certainly if done from an ulterior motive, would be unethical. Other educationalists and social scientists would no doubt identify the methodological inaccuracies, but a non-specialist audience could not necessarily be expected to do so. The latter may perceive the researcher as something of an authority figure, and may be inclined to believe the research results without subjecting them to careful scrutiny.

It may be possible for a researcher to explain some research results in such a way that it suggests a certain course of action, without being explicit. If the intention, and indeed the result here, is that people act in a certain way, perhaps in relation to certain commercial products and services, then this may well be unethical. An atmosphere of research should arguably not be employed in order to make persuasive claims which are either explicitly incorrect, or which might be interpreted in a different manner.

The form of words used in writing about research can sometimes reflect a certainty about the results which is simply not justified by the data. For example, the use of such expressions as 'it is clear that . . .', 'it is obvious that . . .' and 'there is no doubt that . . .' suggests to the reader or listener who is unfamiliar with the interpretation of research findings that the results are fairly definite and clear. This may simply not be so. Other terms which may be inappropriate include statements that 'facts' have been 'uncovered' or 'discovered', and have led to research questions being 'proven'. Many educational and social science researchers will simply regard such expressions as unsuitable within a research report. Nevertheless, if they are used in the context of a non-specialist audience or readership, they may give a misleading impression.

The non-specialist audience may have certain expectations of researchers, in terms of adding to knowledge and helping people to understand the world. They may, by such expectations, put researchers under a subtle form of pressure to be more definite, than is justified by the results. The demands of sound epistemology and of ethical considerations suggest to researchers that they should attempt to indicate the limitations of their findings, and to persuade their audience not to be over-desirous for fixed and rigid formulations of knowledge.

Establishing authorship

One of the most important ethical principles in research procedures is that the grounds for action and decision-making should be transparent and open. Some of the issues involving the authorship of research publications were dealt with in Chapter 7. Although there are a variety of ways of dealing with the issue of, say, multiple authorship, it is important to be open about the principles that are in operation. For example, a journal may have a policy of simply listing multiple authors for an article in alphabetical order of surname, irrespective of any other factors which may be evident. If this is the case, it would be fair to state this policy at some place in the journal; otherwise, some readers may make the assumption that the sequence of authors indicates the magnitude of the contribution to the article.

Sometimes the authorship of a book or research paper may be described as 'author X with author Y.' The use of 'with' rather than 'and' signifies usually that author Y had a secondary role in the writing of the book. However, it is difficult for the reader to understand necessarily the nature of that secondary role. It may be that author Y wrote one or two chapters only, or that they had a generalized role throughout the book. Very often, such a role is specified near the beginning of the book; this is generally a desirable practice.

Sometimes a reader may easily assume that the same named role is identical in two different situations. An example is the role of 'editor'. The role of the editor of an academic journal is different from that of the editor of an academic book. Let us consider the editorial role in the case of an edited book consisting of a series of chapters reporting research, and that of a journal editor. Differences in the editorial role derive from the fact that journal articles are usually unsolicited, whereas the chapters for a research-based book are submitted on invitation. Once the broad theme of a book has been established, the editor seeks out potential contributions that will provide a balanced, integrated volume, which adheres to the predetermined concept. The situation with an academic journal is (as we have discussed) different. In the case of an edited book, the editor may assume a major role in deciding whether or not to accept a chapter which has been submitted, or alternatively a more formal refereeing procedure may be established. Again, it is arguably desirable if the systems being employed are made clear. Readers are then able to form judgements about the status of the research reports in the chapters.

It would be a dull world if there was a complete standardization of procedures in terms of academic journals and other research publications. Whereas procedures may not be the same, it is possible to aspire to a shared degree of openness with which they are described. All those involved in the process, be they authors, editors or readers, can then appreciate the manner in which judgements have been reached about potential publications, and can formulate their own opinions about the value and status of those judgements.

Acting as a reviewer of academic material

The procedures employed in academic journals have been considered earlier in the chapter, but associated with the role of academic reviewer, there are some distinctly ethical questions. Perhaps we could begin by trying to explore whether there is an overarching ethical perspective which may be associated with the role of the reviewer or academic referee. When reviewers receive articles to read, they will usually be asked to form an opinion based on certain criteria. One cannot always be confident that two different reviewers will form the same judgement about an article, however, even though they may be trying to apply the same criteria. For example, one criterion may be that 'the methodology is appropriate to the research aims'. It may be that a variety of approaches could reasonably be expected to investigate and resolve the research aims. One reviewer may be satisfied with the approach that was taken, and let that question rest there. Another reviewer may feel that a different method could have been employed in conjunction with the one that was actually used. Sometimes it is possible to say with a fair degree of certainty that a particular methodology would have been inappropriate given certain research questions or aims. Generally there may be several reasonable options which could have been employed, and one cannot really argue that one methodology was, on its own, wrong or inappropriate. There is an issue about the degree of tolerance which a reviewer can demonstrate.

There may be an ethical stance which a reviewer can take, which involves attempting to place themselves in the position of the author. Such a stance tries to appreciate the difficulties of selecting and then justifying a particular research design. Most researchers and academics tend to understand the relative ease with which it is possible to criticize and critique a research report, if one is so minded. It is a good deal harder to write a good research report than it is to criticize a good research report. If reviewers were to accept this argument, they may feel that they will always hesitate slightly before embarking on a major criticism of a report. This is not to argue for a diminution in standards, but for a more charitable and supportive stance towards articles. It is a question of asking reviewers to try to recall their own feelings of uncertainty when they have written research articles and reports. This is an ethical stance because it is concerned with trying to empathize with the feelings of others, and with the difficulties which they experience.

At the end of the day, the reviewer has to make a decision and should apply the criteria advocated by the publication concerned. However, there is a certain scope for judgement, and that is the area within which this particular style of ethical perspective operates. It is a perspective which is concerned with empathy for others, with trying to appreciate the feelings and uncertainties of others, with a fundamental sympathy for others, and above all with trying if possible to support the efforts of others within the parameters of the authority one is given. None of this is to deny any of the important functions of the reviewer, but to explore the ethical dimensions of the manner in which these tasks may be approached.

Other aspects of being sensitive to the author are for the reviewer to provide a speedy reply and to give clear guidance on the ways in which the article has (if such should be the case) been perceived to fall short of the standards required. It can be helpful if journals have a policy on the time-scale for providing feedback to authors. Ideally this policy should be agreed with reviewers and published in the journal, specifying the maximum time period for which an author should have to wait before receiving a review. If an article does require amendments, the reviewer's comments should clearly specify the changes needed to lift the standard of the article to that required for publication. If the article is being rejected outright, the reviewer should indicate the broad strategies required to provide a better chance for the article to be accepted by another journal.

The uses of synopses of research

Synopses and abstracts play a significant role in the dissemination of research. They may often be the first point of contact for a reader or another researcher who wishes to gain a rapid grasp of the contents of a research report or article. It is often good practice to attach to the abstract a list of the key concepts which are included in the research study. In the case of a very long research study, readers may not wish to invest the time to read the whole article without being fairly certain that it is related to their own research interests. The inclusion of a list of key concepts enables the reader to grasp at a glance the main cognitive aspects of the study. These key concepts may also be used to catalogue, classify or index research studies in databases. It is hence important that they genuinely reflect the contents of the research report.

The only ethical issues in connection with the abstract of a research study are to remember that the abstract is written for the benefit of others. Its purpose is to provide a precis of the research, rather than to revisit the more complex discussion in the thesis or report. The abstract should be as accurate as possible; it should summarize the principal features of the research design, without repeating the various justifications for using that approach. It should provide an overview of the data-collection and analysis techniques, without providing any of the detailed discussion which would normally be provided in the full research account. It is important that the abstract is clear, but also that it provides a balanced picture of the results. It is far more desirable from a research viewpoint to err on the side of caution, rather than to exaggerate the results in any way, or to make claims which cannot be readily substantiated.

There is generally no need to repeat any of the questions which might have been in the researcher's mind during the research, particularly where the author raises rhetorical questions to indicate the broad areas with which the research has been concerned. It is more informative for the reader if the abstract is restricted to affirming the main results and to indicating the limitations of those results. Above all, the abstract should be helpful to the reader, conveying the main outcomes of the research, and providing guidance as to whether this research is relevant to their areas of interest.

Acknowledging the limitations of research conclusions

It is important that researchers try to be as balanced, objective and accurate as they can in reporting the results of research and in drawing conclusions. Being accurate entails the capacity to appreciate the possible limitations to accuracy. The ethical issues here are similar to those inherent in the accurate expression of academic judgements, for example in terms of the influence which research results have on society in general, and the importance therefore of expressing conclusions in a valid manner.

There are many factors limiting the extent to which researchers can feel a degree of certainty towards their conclusions. The sample may not have been sufficiently large, or may have had to be adapted in some way because of the practicalities of the research. This in turn may have had an impact upon any statistical methods used. In the case of qualitative data, there is always an element of selectivity in the data which are actually collected for analysis. Researchers usually collect more data than they can usefully incorporate in their analysis, which entails the selection of some data and the rejection of others. The researcher should be as clear as possible about the grounds and criteria for this selection, and make these criteria clear when presenting the research conclusions. Researchers can also have a considerable impact on the nature of the qualitative data collected, simply because of their presence and influence. This effect may be particularly significant in the case of interview research. Both the questions which are asked in unstructured interviews and the manner in which they are asked can affect the kinds of responses which are obtained. It is becoming increasingly common for researchers to provide a reflective account as part of the conclusion of a research report, in order to explore the manner in which their own perspective on the world may have influenced the collection and analysis of data (Seale 1999: 159–77).

The original design of the research project can influence the conclusions. The manner in which the research aims are expressed and conceptualized will affect the whole progress of the research. The choice of methodology reflects to some extent the approach of the researchers. It may be possible, for example, to address the same aims by using several different methodological approaches, and it is here that the subjective conceptions of the researchers may make themselves felt. The researchers should do their best to analyse these personal conceptions which may have influenced the progress of the research, and reflect upon the manner in which they might have affected the way in which the conclusions were drawn.

It is difficult to imagine research as an exclusively linear process which starts with research questions and aims, and progresses inexorably and logically to a conclusion. It seems much more frequently to have a significantly random element consisting of unanticipated outcomes and unexpected turns of event. It is also a process which contains many opportunities for choices to be made. Such choices may be between different research designs, different methodologies and different forms of analysis. It is, in fact, a process which may be surprisingly subjective, and there is, it can be argued, a moral demand upon researchers to try to examine and explain this subjectivity to the consumers of research.

9　Conclusion
The role of the researcher

Representation of research findings to non-researchers

Researchers may have all kinds of reasons for participating in research. They may be following an educational programme in which research is an important component. They may regard research as a high status activity which can have a positive impact on their career prospects. They may have a passionate interest in some element of their subject, and wish to explore it further and add to the total of knowledge in that area. They may wish to bring benefit to humanity, through new scientific discoveries or through a better understanding of social processes. Researchers may be motivated by a combination of these and other factors.

Part of our concept of research may well be that we wish to use it to enhance the world, and to add something to the quality of life of other people. Now it may be possible to achieve such an end and still not to communicate the details of the research to those who benefit from it. For example, we might use our research findings to develop a new form of medication to treat an illness, and simply distribute the new treatment. However, we may feel that it is part of the ethics of the situation not only to distribute the practical benefits which emanate from the research, but also to distribute at least a summary of the key research results. The latter could be achieved in an accessible form of language. We may wish to do this because we would like to involve people more in the process of advancing knowledge and this seems the most appropriate method. We may also wish to involve people more in understanding the benefits of research, and the most appropriate method again seems to be to explain the essence of the particular findings. To do anything other may perhaps appear to be rather patronizing, in the sense that it simply relates the benefits of research, without explaining the origin of those benefits. Much of this approach is concerned with the motives inherent in research, and the justifications we adopt for carrying out certain kinds of actions. Let us examine the issue of ethical motives further in Box 9.1.

Box 9.1   Theoretical perspective: ethical motives

When we speak of motives in ethics we are to some extent emphasizing the intentions of a human being in relation to an ethical dilemma, and the way in which those intentions reflect the inward nature of that human being. At the same time, we are minimizing our concerns with the results of actions. Discussion of motives is a discussion of the way in which our internal nature manifests itself in certain behavioural acts. On this model, these acts are largely impelled by our view that such acts are the right thing to do under those circumstances. Although we may reflect upon the possible consequences, these are not pre-eminent in our decision-making. We do what we do, because our powers of rational moral analysis tell us that such an action is ethically correct (see Von Wright 1963: 209).

It is part of our motive as a researcher not only to add to knowledge, but also to pass on and share such new knowledge with others. We may feel that to restrict new contributions to knowledge to a limited few is generally unacceptable, and that it is morally desirable to share knowledge wherever possible. On this view, we are less concerned with the ultimate ends of such an action (although these may be desirable), but simply with the virtues of the strategy itself.

Recognition of the value of different research methodologies

Most researchers probably have their own favourite research methodology. Some people feel happier working with quantitative data, while others have a natural affiliation for words. It is desirable that researchers, like other professionals, try to emphasize their strengths. However, this should not prevent them seeing the value inherent in other approaches. They may not necessarily use such approaches in their own research, but an understanding of other perspectives is arguably important from a number of different points of view.

Researchers do need to keep up to date in their specialist subject area, which entails reading widely in the research literature. Usually this will require the assimilation of research reports utilizing a range of methodologies and types of data analyses. An appreciation of the contribution which different methodologies can make to research in a particular subject is thus desirable. Equally well, if a researcher is placed in the position of advising a colleague, or perhaps of supervising a research student, a familiarity with a range of perspectives is useful. If one accepts that the nature of the research questions or aims largely condition the type of methodology which is appropriate, providing advice to research students generally necessitates a familiarity with a broad range of possible research designs. Each research student will formulate research questions in different ways depending upon their particular con-cept of the research problem. If a research supervisor were always to suggest directing the research in such a way that their own particular favoured methodology could be used, this would result in rather narrow and pre-dictable advice. It would seem preferable to let the research student define the nature of the research question, and then to explore in discussion the types of appropriate methodologies.

Social research is, in its broadest terms, about exploring the world, about examining the nature of human existence, and of the relationship between different human beings in society. So complex are the variables in such an enterprise, that one requires as multifaceted an approach as possible. It appears that the researcher can aspire to this task only by being as open as possible in terms of methodology, utilizing every possible perspective which can explore the nature of the human condition. The antithesis of this is the closed approach to methodology, where the researcher predetermines their favoured methodology, and then tries to adopt this approach in as many circumstances as possible. Now with a careful selection of research questions, it may be feasible to do this, although it will necessitate a very careful matching of research problem and perspective. If this approach is employed by supervisors in relation to research students, it may be restrictive of the latter, in the sense that they may in effect have a rather limited choice of research questions. It does appear that there is almost an ethical issue here about the nature of research and the role of the researcher, in terms of being as open as possible, both towards the definition of research problems, and also to the selection of research paradigms within which to work. To put it another way, it is perhaps a question of allowing the social world to define the issues which need investi-gating and the way in which this should be done, rather than the researcher preselecting the paradigm, and then searching around for problems which fit that approach.

Consultation with peers on complex ethical issues

Ethical issues in education and the social sciences are so complex that once one starts to analyse the ethical issues inherent in a particular research project, one often feels that the debate could go on and on for ever. One could easily get into a position where one would never feel confident in starting the research! There is probably a point in any research project where researchers feel that they have done their best to address the principal ethical issues, and that they are simply going to proceed in good faith. Let us consider the complex dilemma described in Box 9.2.

Box 9.2 Ethical dilemma: the extent of ethical issues
Two researchers decide that they would like to investigate the difficulties experienced by high school students who feel that they do not easily make friends at school and hence are unhappy. Many feel socially isolated and lonely; in some cases this has a deleterious effect upon their school work. It also can lead to students being absent from school for considerable periods. The researchers feel that their research might eventually help such young people. However, they are concerned about the large number of potential ethical issues, for example by talking to the students they may cause them to relive unhappy experiences, and they are also concerned that their research might make it seem that these students were being treated differently. They are also aware that the attitudes of parents may differ. Some may welcome the research, while others may feel that it is intrusive. The researchers wonder whether some students may not wish to participate because they feel that it draws attention to their difficulties. The researchers are not certain whether they can resolve these issues.

This situation is complex from an ethical point of view. It might be possible to identify potential respondents based upon the perceptions of teachers, but it could be difficult to approach such students and ask them if they were unhappy at school. Some students may deny this, while others may be upset that their difficulties have been identified. This could result in their being even more unhappy. It may well be both desirable and necessary to consult parents concerning research of this nature, and they may feel ambivalent about the research.

In such a situation it is understandable that the researchers are concerned about the ethical issues. A possibility here would be to design the research so that it explored in general terms the way in which different students adjusted to social life at school. Hence, the teachers could be asked to identify a sample of students, some of whom seemed to be happy and well adjusted at school, and others who were to varying degrees less happy and perhaps less well socially integrated. All of the students could then be interviewed, without the appearance of having selected any one particular sub-group. It might be possible to ask questions in such a manner that even those who were less happy at school would not feel disturbed. For example, all the students could be asked about those aspects of the social life of the school which they enjoyed, and those aspects which they did not enjoy. Parents may also feel generally happy about such a research design, because it does not identify any particular sub-group for special treatment.

Even though this research design may appear to have overcome many of the researchers' original concerns, it may still be beneficial to consult peers about the ethical issues. Peers might include the teachers at the school, including the senior staff and headteacher, other researchers, and academic staff in the institution at which the researchers are based. Peers may not be able to actually resolve or eliminate all of the ethical issues and problems within a research design, but they can provide other important advantages. They can provide reassurance about the strategies which the researcher has decided to use, and can advise whether any supplementary action might be contemplated. They can also advise whether in their view all reasonable steps have been taken in terms of ethical issues. Finally, and perhaps most importantly, in the light of their review of the research project, they can advise whether on balance, they feel the researchers should proceed with the project. This will probably rarely be to say that the project is perfect from an ethical point of view, but at least that it has been sufficiently well designed, within the terms of what is currently accepted as reasonable within the broad research and educational community.

Using forms of communication and language which are appropriate to the context

The researcher has a moral responsibility in terms of reporting their research accurately and in a style of writing which is accessible to the reader. As there are different outlets for research, it may be that the researcher will need to adjust the style of writing for different contexts. Nevertheless, the style of writing and communication should be capable of conveying the key issues of the research. In a popular, non-academic journal, the style should not be so simplistic that it fails to convey the essentials of the research design and the conclusions. In a highly academic journal, it is no virtue to write in a convoluted style, using academic jargon in such a way that the meaning is obscured. The ultimate purpose of writing about research is to communicate the findings so that others may set the research in the context of previous work in the field, seek to replicate the research, or perhaps use the research as a basis for further work.

Very often in research, data may be interpreted in a number of different ways. Arguably, this is especially the case with qualitative data, where the researcher often makes a selection from a broad range of data, and then chooses to interpret that selection in a particular way. It is important to at least indicate in the research report that there are alternatives in terms of the analysis. The ethical aspects of this are that the rather less experienced reader may assume that there is only one way of analysing the data, and therefore may gain a rather too rigid and limiting grasp of the research area. When the researcher indicates that there are alternatives, this may well give the student or less-experienced reader the confidence to reflect on the data themselves, and to carry out their own analysis.

It is perhaps more the case with research in education and the social sciences, that the researcher has a great wealth of perspectives to choose from when conducting research. These range from phenomenology to ethnography to interactionism and positivism. When researchers are making a selection of perspective, they are typically influenced by a variety of factors. These may range from, for example, a natural affinity with numerical data, or a preference for data resulting from individual, subjective reflection. They will also be influenced by the nature of the research subject. The choice of perspective, and the way in which that approach is operationalized in the research, will also depend upon other factors in the intellectual history of the researcher. This is at least one of the aspects which has encouraged researchers to write reflexive or reflective accounts to accompany their research. Reflective accounts are often written in the first person, and try to present, in an albeit subjective manner, an analysis of the way in which the intellectual back-ground of the researcher may have interacted with the way in which the research was conducted. Such an account does not treat the research process as an entity which is given, but rather as something which is created through an interaction between the particular worldview of the researcher and the selected research question. The use of the first person and of an auto-biographical style does tend to emphasize to the reader the fact that there is an element in research which very much reflects the personal decision-making of the researcher. The slight but no doubt tangible ethical issue is that this can tend to give confidence to the less experienced researcher, to reflect on their own preferences in research methodology and to have confidence in articulating those preferences. Arguably, the most important issue here is that researchers are aware of the reflexivity operating in the research process, and are able to analyse that process and place it in a coherent written form within the public domain.

The benefits and disadvantages of being a research participant

It is a widely used ethical principle that one should try to understand how the other person feels. This is often extremely difficult. We may try to remember how we felt under similar circumstances, but there may be many circum-stances of which we have never had experience. In any case, people react in different ways to circumstances. It is thus not always easy to appreciate the feelings of others in certain contexts. Nevertheless, it is a useful exercise in terms of trying to understand how we might act ethically towards others.

It is certainly easy for researchers to become so involved with their research that there is a tendency to forget to some extent the situation of the respondents. It is an interesting ethical principle that researchers should not only consider the desirability or otherwise of the ends of a research project, but also reflect on the advantages and disadvantages for the research participants.

A number of possible strategies might be adopted. During interview research for example, participants could be invited to discuss issues of concern to them. Even though the researcher may have an interview schedule and a list of topics to raise, perhaps time can be set aside to invite the participant to add items to the interview agenda. This may help them feel that they are much more involved in the research process, and not simply providing data on questions which have been unilaterally determined. When postal questionnaires are distributed, participants could be invited to contact the research team about any issues relevant to the questionnaire. This could be accomplished by phone or electronically. The purpose need not be to collect further data, but merely to give participants an opportunity to enter into a dialogue.

In case study or ethnographic research, it may be possible to provide some feedback to members of the research setting, in order to engage in an exchange of views on the research. For example, in an ethnographic study of a school department, it may be possible to arrange a meeting with the departmental staff to discuss the progress of the research from the researcher's point of view, and to give the teachers an opportunity to discuss the research from a participant's perspective. This may enable them to learn from the research experience, rather than merely having the opportunity to read a research report or thesis, which may be some considerable time in preparation. The learning experience is more immediate, and treats them much more as participants than as research subjects.

Another possibility in terms of helping participants to gain something from the research experience is to discuss with them ways in which they could become involved in inquiries as researchers. Teachers, for example, may have an interest in doing this, perhaps in the form of action research studies, but not be quite certain how they could convert their research ideas into practice. Some may enrol on part-time courses of study; others may wish to consider small-scale studies with a view to publication, but are unsure how to embark on such research. Advice from practitioner-researchers could help them turn such aspirations into reality.

There may be other advantages and positive features of being involved in the research process. Participants may simply enjoy having someone being interested in their opinions and valuing what they have to say. This may give people confidence and enhance their self-esteem. The research process may help them to look at their own situation in a different light, and to learn from the process of reflection. Overall, there does seem to be an important ethical issue in researchers giving careful thought to ways of maximizing the enjoyment, satisfaction and learning gained by participants in the research process.

Some principles for trying to resolve ethical dilemmas in research

We have examined a range of ethical dilemmas and issues, and explored theoretical approaches which might help in analysing these issues. Some of these theoretical perspectives have taken the form of proposed general rules for ethical decision-making. There may be a feeling that although these can be helpful in trying to resolve dilemmas, there is perhaps no single rule which is entirely satisfactory in this regard; it can be argued that ethical issues are fundamentally different in nature from empirical issues. Ethical issues may in effect be propositions about how the world ought to be, whereas empirical propositions are about how the world is. In the case of empirical propositions, it may be somewhat evident how we could proceed in terms of falsifying the proposition, but in the case of ethical propositions, this may be much less clear.

Thus, if someone proposes that a person should behave in a certain sort of way in the future, or that the world ought to be a particular kind of place, we may feel that there are limited empirical data which are relevant in helping us to support or negate the proposition. One practical way in which we seek to resolve ethical questions is to immediately turn to the way in which people have acted in the past. For example, if we were concerned whether it was acceptable to interview primary age children for a research project, we could turn to recent research studies to see whether this has been done before. We might then read reports and articles to ascertain whether there had been any undesirable consequences. We might ask primary school teachers and our researcher colleagues for their opinion.

In effect, what we would be doing here is trying to ascertain the norms and values which are accepted in current society. In a sense, our implicit line of reasoning would be that if it was typically sanctioned in society in the recent past, and if it is accepted generally now, then it is also acceptable for ourselves. This is a common form of decision-making, but it has a number of disadvantages. Such a logic cannot argue that an action is morally right, only that lots of people do it. We can all think of activities in which a great many people engage, but which some individuals would feel to be unethical. Hence the number of people involved in an activity says very little about whether it is ethically correct. However, in the context of research, where generally researchers are trying to act responsibly, the fact that many people behave according to a certain norm is a reasonable guide to the moral desirability of a particular action.

As a different strategy, we might try to apply some of the rules and formulations which are an evident part of much ethical theorizing. Some of the theories explored in this book may be reduced to short maxims which attempt to provide guidance in a wide range of specific circumstances. However, situations do vary enormously; sometimes the attempt to apply an ethical rule results in an artificiality of decision-making. Besides this, there is the issue of which rule or theoretical position to take. As we have seen, the application of different rules and theories may lead to very different decisions. Nevertheless, some researchers may find it very useful to adopt a particular ethical perspective, such as always trying to evaluate the consequences of ethical decisions in order to try to ensure that the greatest good results. The use of such formulations has the advantage that the researcher knows that at least some well-established ethical principles will be used in the decision-making, even if not necessarily all factors are taken into account through this approach. Similarly, the application of ethical rules has the added advantage that it is about as straightforward as any ethical decision-making can be, and may result in a fairly rapid decision. Nonetheless, situations alter, and situations are not all the same. Rules are thus unlikely to provide a general means of making sound ethical decisions, but they remain something to which many researchers have recourse when making decisions.

So if neither the use of societal norms as a guide, nor the application of rules and formulations can provide a certain means of resolving ethical problems in research, perhaps we can conclude by examining one further approach which may help us. This approach starts from the premise that since ethical dilemmas are all different, even though some may appear to have elements in common, we do need a method which is sufficiently flexible to take into account the great variety of situations. Indeed this approach is usually known as situation or situationist ethics. Let us look at the rather more theoretical model of this approach and then consider how it could be applied to a research context (see Box 9.3).

It may help us, in applying this perspective to research, to use an alternative word to love. When using this concept, situation ethicists have in mind an approach based on a deep sense of caring for one's fellow human beings. We might want to use concepts such as empathy, deep affection or caring for the welfare of others. However we actually conceptualize this, the perspective is concerned with our placing the humanity and welfare of others at the centre of our considerations. If we think of it in those terms, we can more easily apply it to research contexts.

Suppose we are planning some research to develop strategies to help those who have been unemployed for long periods of time. As we are planning our research we begin to think of the ways in which we might identify our sample, and the kinds of questions we might ask the research participants. We begin to wonder whether there might be any ethical issues in research of this kind, for example adverse effects for those being interviewed. According to a situation ethics perspective, we should be predominantly concerned with the welfare of the possible participants. We should not be concerned with the articles that

---

Box 9.3   Theoretical perspective: situation ethics

The perspective of situation ethics takes the view that each ethical dilemma or decision is different. Part of the reason for this is the emphasis given to the uniqueness of each human being, and therefore the singular dimension this brings to each ethical decision. It is partly this individualistic perspective which causes situation ethics to tend to regard the application of general rules in ethics as inappropriate. In terms of reaching a decision on an ethical issue, situation ethics stresses the importance of acting out of love for the people involved in the issue. It is felt that if a person is acting out of genuine love for others, then the correct ethical decision will emerge from those feelings and motivation. One of the fundamental ideas of this approach is that it is based upon a feeling of deep empathy for the people involved. In addition, it is felt that whereas one cannot predetermine exactly the decision which will be taken in any situation, if it is motivated by the desire to love and value others, then it will ultimately be a moral decision (see Johnstone 1994: 82).

---

we might write, or the official reports we produce, or even particularly with the social policy strategies we might formulate. The problem with the latter is that we cannot know whether they might be implemented, or even if they were implemented, whether they would be successful in helping unemployed people. All we do know is that we are planning to involve some people in research who may feel somewhat uncertain and vulnerable through having been out of work for some time. Our whole concern should be with thinking about their welfare, attempting to ensure that the research is not disturbing for them, and trying to treat them with as much care and respect as possible. If we can do that, and if we can keep those feelings and motives at the forefront of our minds at all times, then according to the situation ethics perspective, we should hopefully make the correct ethical decisions in relation to the research. If we lose sight of that priority, and if we allow the welfare of the participants to move from the centrality of our concerns, then our moral decision-making will no longer be certain. We will have lost something of our true value system. We should, according to this view, always place our fellow human beings at the very heart of our concerns. It is true that our ethical decision-making may not always be consistent; it is true that different people may vary in their decisions in comparable circumstances; and it is even true that the same person may make different decisions in apparently comparable circumstances; but the argument is that the decisions will always have a strong moral element to them.

There are many things apparently wrong with situation ethics. It is a perspective which is very subjective; it may lead to rapid and ill-considered decisions; it may result in inconsistent decisions; and it could be adapted by some to seek to justify completely inappropriate actions. However, it is a perspective which takes us right back to arguably the heart of ethical concerns. It takes us back to the idea of trying our best to love and care for all our fellow human beings. If we always aspire to that in research, we will not go far wrong.

References

Aldridge, A. and Levine, K. (2001) *Surveying the Social World: Principles and Practice in Survey Research*. Buckingham: Open University Press.

Brown, M., Boyle, B. and Boyle, T. (2000) The shared management role of the head of department in English secondary schools, *Research in Education*, 63: 33–47.

Bryman, A. (2001) *Social Research Methods*. Oxford: Oxford University Press.

Burns, R.B. (2000) *Introduction to Research Methods*. London: Sage.

Cameron, J.E. and Lalonde, R.N. (2001) Social identification and gender-related ideology in women and men, *British Journal of Social Psychology*, 40: 59–77.

Creswell, J.W. (1998) *Qualitative Inquiry and Research Design: Choosing Among Five Traditions*. London: Sage.

Crow, I. (2000) The power of research, in D. Burton (ed.) *Research Training for Social Scientists: A Handbook for Postgraduate Researchers*. London: Sage.

Davis, N.A. (1993) Contemporary deontology, in P. Singer (ed.) *A Companion to Ethics*. Oxford: Blackwell.

Denscombe, M. (2001) Uncertain identities and health-risking behaviour: the case of young people and smoking in late modernity, *British Journal of Sociology*, 52: 157–77.

Eriksen, T.H. (1997) Ethnicity, race and nation, in M. Guibernau and J. Rex (eds) *The Ethnicity Reader: Nationalism, Multiculturalism and Migration*. Cambridge: Polity.

Fenton, S. (1999) *Ethnicity, Class and Culture*. London: Macmillan.

Fielding, N. (1993) Ethnography, in N. Gilbert (ed.) *Researching Social Life*. London: Sage.

Frankena, W.K. (1967) The naturalistic fallacy, in P. Foot (ed.) *Theories of Ethics*. Oxford: Oxford University Press.

Gilbert, N. (1993) Writing about social research, in N. Gilbert (ed.) *Researching Social Life*. London: Sage.

Greig, A. and Taylor, J. (1999) *Doing Research with Children*. London: Sage.

Hudson, W.D. (1970) *Modern Moral Philosophy*. London: Macmillan.

Husted, G.L. and Husted, J.H. (1995) *Ethical Decision-making in Nursing*. St Louis, MO: Mosby.

Jackson, R. and Nesbitt, E. (1993) *Hindu Children in Britain*. Stoke-on-Trent: Trentham.

Johnstone, M-J. (1994) *Bioethics: A Nursing Perspective*. Sydney: Harcourt Brace.

Kane, E. (1995) *Doing Your Own Research: Basic Descriptive Research in the Social Sciences and Humanities*. London: Marion Boyars.

Knight, P.T. (2002) *Small-scale Research*. London: Sage.

Kvale, S. (1996) *Interviews: An Introduction to Qualitative Research Interviewing*. Thousand Oaks, CA: Sage.

Loewy, E.H. (1996) *Textbook of Healthcare Ethics*. New York: Plenum.

Mackie, J.L. (1977) *Ethics: Inventing Right and Wrong*. Harmondsworth: Penguin.

Maykut, P. and Morehouse, R. (1994) *Beginning Qualitative Research*. London: Falmer.

Middlewood, D., Coleman, M. and Lumby, J. (1999) *Practitioner Research in Education: Making a Difference*. London: Paul Chapman.

Nielson, K. (1998) Traditional morality and utilitarianism, in J.P. Sterba (ed.) *Ethics: The Big Questions*. Oxford: Blackwell.

O'Neill, O. (1993) Kantian ethics, in P. Singer (ed.) *A Companion to Ethics*. Oxford: Blackwell.

Punch, K.F. (1998) *Introduction to Social Research: Quantitative and Qualitative Approaches*. London: Sage.

Railton, P. (1998) Alienation, consequentialism, and the demands of morality, in J.P. Sterba (ed.) *Ethics: The Big Questions*. Oxford: Blackwell.

Raphael, D.D. (1981) *Moral Philosophy*. Oxford: Oxford University Press.

Richardson, L. (1994) Writing: a method of inquiry, in N.K. Denzin and Y.S. Lincoln (eds) *Handbook of Qualitative Research*. Thousand Oaks, CA: Sage.

Ross, W.D. (1964) *Aristotle*. London: Methuen.

Schutt, R.K. (1996) *Investigating the Social World: The Process and Practice of Research*. Thousand Oaks, CA: Pine Forge.

Seale, C. (1999) *The Quality of Qualitative Research*. London: Sage.

Shaffir, W.B. and Stebbins, R.A. (1991) Introduction, in W.B. Shaffir and R.A. Stebbins (eds) *Experiencing Fieldwork: An Inside View of Qualitative Research*. Newbury Park, CA: Sage.

Stangor, C. (1998) *Research Methods for the Behavioural Sciences*. Boston, MA: Houghton Mifflin.

Townend, D.M.R. (2000) Can the law prescribe an ethical framework for social science research? in D. Burton (ed.) *Research Training for Social Scientists*. London: Sage.

Van Kammen, W.B. and Stouthamer-Loeber, M. (1998) Practical aspects of interview data collection and data management, in L. Bickman and D.J. Rog (eds) *Handbook of Applied Social Research Methods*. Thousand Oaks, CA: Sage.

Von Wright, G.H. (1963) *The Varieties of Goodness*. London: Routledge and Kegan Paul.

Wattenmaker, W.D. (2000) Domains and knowledge effects: strategies in object and social classification, *American Journal of Psychology*, 113: 405–29.

Index

LEARNING FROM RESEARCH
GETTING MORE FROM YOUR DATA

Judith Bell and Clive Opie

- How do I begin to plan my research?
- How can I be sure that I am collecting useful data and analysing it appropriately?
- Do I need a sophisticated understanding of statistics in order to carry out high quality research?

If these are questions which concern you, then you will find great support in this reassuring and down to earth book. It tells the story of five postgraduate researchers on their journey to successful completion of Master of Education or PhD degrees. Four of the five were new to research, had demanding full time jobs and so were researching part time – and at a distance. All four undertook quantitative studies and even though two of them claimed to be 'afraid of stats' at the beginning, they all succeeded in producing quality theses. The fifth researcher had previous relevant research experience and had an award which enabled her to carry out a full time qualitative investigation at doctoral level. All five faced sharp learning curves at various times but they learned from their experiences, as we all do. They discuss very openly some of the mistakes they made, the lessons they learned and, with hindsight, how they might have done things differently.

A comprehensive glossary, key quotations in boxes and detailed annotated further reading combined with a straightforward writing style make this an invaluable text for any researcher.

Contents
Acknowledgements – Introduction – Part one: The descriptive study – Background to the study and critics of descriptive studies – The preparation – Moving on to data collection – Using computer statistical packages – Part two: The evaluation study – Background to the study, obtaining permission and reviewing the literature – The preparation – Operationalization of the concepts – The questionnaire – The findings – Part three: The experimental study – Background to the study – The literature review – Obtaining permission and ethical dilemmas in experimental research – Aims and purpose of the study – The plan for data collection and analysis – The results – Part four: The ethnographic study – Statement of the problem and purpose of the study – Setting the scene and the analysis of documentary evidence – The review of the literature – The research contract and the principle of informed consent – The fieldwork – Analysing the data – A solution to the problem? – Part five: The survey – Background to the study – The preparation and the planning – The staff questionnaire – Discussion of the findings – Glossary – References – Index.

288pp   0 335 20660 3 (Paperback)   0 335 20661 1 (Hardback)

HOW TO RESEARCH

Loraine Blaxter, Christina Hughes and Malcolm Tight

Praise for the first edition:

> . . . an immensely useful resource.
>
> *Nursing Times Research*

> As a graduate research student, I have come across a number of books claiming to inform the reader 'how to research', and have become sceptical . . . This book challenges that sceptism and is to be warmly welcomed.
>
> *Research Policy and Planning*

> . . . an excellent choice for any student about to start a research project for the first time.
>
> *British Journal of Educational Technology*

How to Research 2nd Edition is about the practice and experience of doing research in the social sciences as well as in related subjects such as education, business studies and health and social care. It is aimed at those, particularly the less experienced, who are involved in small-scale research projects at college or at work. The book is written in an original, accessible and jargon-free style using a variety of different forms of presentation to support the researcher.

How to Research 2nd Edition offers:

- a series of useful exercises to help progress research thinking
- a wide range of examples taken from a variety of subject areas
- extensive annotated bibliographies for further reading
- practical hints for all stages of the research process

This new edition has been completely revised with up-to-date bibliographies and has new sections on choosing the appropriate method; internet research; and searching the internet.

It will be a core text for undergraduate and postgraduate research methods courses in the social sciences and will also be invaluable for those carrying out research as part of a workplace assignment.

Contents
Thinking about research – Getting started – Thinking about methods – Reading for research – Managing your project – Collecting data – Analysing data – Writing up – Finishing off – References – Index.

304pp   0 335 20903 3 (Paperback)   0 335 21121 6 (Hardback)

GROUND RULES FOR GOOD RESEARCH
A 10 POINT GUIDE FOR SOCIAL RESEARCHERS

Martyn Denscombe

This book provides a user-friendly starting point for people doing small-scale social research projects. It identifies the key ideas and practices that underlie good research and provides clear guidelines to help newcomers and experienced researchers alike to design and conduct projects which meet the basic criteria for success.

It is written for undergraduate, postgraduate and professional students in business studies, social sciences, health studies, media studies and education who need to undertake research projects as part of their studies. It will also prove invaluable for professionals with little experience of research.

Key features of the book include:

- The identification of 10 ground rules for good social research
- Checklists to help researchers evaluate their approach and avoid fundamental errors
- A clear and jargon free style
- Attractive presentation with plenty of useful lists and summaries, text boxes and key points

Contents
Introduction – Foundations for research – Purpose – Relevance – Resources – Originality – Accuracy – Accountability – Generalizations – Objectivity – Ethics – Proof – References – Index.

224pp   0 335 20651 4 (Paperback)   0 335 20652 2 (Hardback)